The White Rose and the Swastika

by

Jutta Marshall

Highgate of Beverley

Highgate Publications (Beverley) Limited
2000

ACKNOWLEDGEMENTS

I would like to thank the following, without whose help the publication of this book would have remained a dream:

Ken Forster, Frederick E. Smith, Moe Sherrard-Smith, Bill Spence, Ces Mowthorpe and other friends from the Scarborough Writers' Circle and Scarborough Writers' Weekend for their guidance and expert advice.

My Austrian relatives and friends: Karl and Christiane Schweighofer, Inge and Helmut Klammer, Eva Paulhart, Gerda Seibt, Helga Buhl, Hedy and Oliver Österreicher and Eva Fichtinger for their contributions to the research for and illustration of the book.

And my husband, Brian, and sons, Martin and Robert, for their technical expertise and general support.

British Library Cataloguing in Publication Data.
A catalogue record for this book is available from the British Library.

© 2000 Jutta Marshall
Juta Marshall asserts the moral right to be identified as the author of this work.

ISBN 1 902645 14 6

Published by

Highgate of Beverley

Highgate Publications (Beverley) Limited
4 Newbegin, Beverley, HU17 8EG. Telephone (01482) 886017

Produced by

4 Newbegin, Beverley, HU17 8EG. Telephone (01482) 886017

**In loving memory of Omi,
my grandma in a million.**

To Bernard with best wishes

Julie Marshall

Jan 2013

CONTENTS

PROLOGUE

A sudden gust straight from the North Sea had whirled a few untimely snowflakes into the hallway of our Scarborough home. It was in the early hours of 31 March 1989, our Silver Wedding day, and the last guests had just departed. Elated and exhausted I had sunk into a comfortable chair. I needed to unwind a little, to reflect on twenty-five very happy years of my life. From empty champagne bottles my eyes wandered to what was left of the celebration cake, then to the numerous cards and presents Brian and I had received. The most original gift and our declared favourite, the symbolic white rose tree, had already found a special place in our garden. I smiled, remembering the message on the attached card: 'To a dear Yorkshire couple on twenty-five years of togetherness'.

Unlike my husband and his family I was not born or bred in Yorkshire, far from it. I'd spent my childhood in the Ostmark of Hitler's Third Reich and my teens in Allied-occupied post-war Austria. My introduction to Britain only came in 1961, when I attended a London summer school. A chance visit to the North-East had made me fall in love with Yorkshire's scenic coastline and a certain young Yorkshireman called Brian Marshall. At Easter 1964 all my dreams came true. It was just like the fairy tales my grandma used to tell me when I was a little girl: 'She married her handsome prince and they lived happily ever after.'

In reality, following my prince to a distant land was not without problems. From the Vienna Woods to the North Sea shores, from German to English with that strange Yorkshire accent, from metric shillings, metres and grams to imperial pounds, feet and ounces, from Wiener Schnitzel and Apfelstrudel to Yorkshire Pudding and tea with milk – the contrasts were vast and sometimes daunting. But the kind Yorkshire folk, above all Brian and his lovely mum, took the foreign girl straight to their hearts and made her most welcome in their midst.

Even Mama and Papa, resentful over losing their only child to a stranger whose language they didn't understand, eventually relented to the charm of their son-in-law and his fellow-countrymen. And when Baby Martin came along, his parents' and grandparents' happiness was complete. For Martin, now twenty-four, the party was a good excuse to leave his desk in London and head back north. His younger brother, a student at Hull University and lodging in nearby Beverley, was still in easy reach of the family home. Robert wouldn't have missed this weekend for the world, as he himself had reason to celebrate: narrowly failing to become his parents' fifth anniversary 'bad planning' which made him an April Fool's baby.

'How quickly our babies have grown up,' I mused, watching my boys cheerfully getting to grips with the party's aftermath. Having polished off the last crumbs of their mother's Austrian cakes they finally disappeared to their rooms. It was time I retired, too. Only a few hours and work would start again in our Scarborough family business.

'Thank you for all the love, support and happiness you've given me, dear,' I whispered snuggling up to Brian: 'There's to another twenty-five wonderful years together!'

ONE

THE BIG, BLACK SPIDER AND THE MAN WITH THE LITTLE MOUSTACHE

I woke very early on that September morning in 1940 and nearly choked on my breakfast roll. This was it, the day I had been looking forward to with such excitement, my first day at school.

'There is my big schoolgirl now!' Making a final adjustment to the straps of my brand-new satchel Mama placed a reassuring arm around my shoulders.

Then we were heading for the tall, yellow building next to the church. Listening to the rattle of slate and wooden pencil case in my back satchel I skipped along, making the string-attached sponge and rag fly behind me like little kites. But the skipping turned into a dragging of feet as we approached the school and, panic-stricken, I gripped Mama's hand tightly. The door with the big number one opened and I found myself in a vast, austere room with two long rows of wooden desks-cum-benches. Most of the front wall was covered by a red-and-white flag with a big, black spider in the centre. It was draped round the picture of a man wearing a uniform and a strange little moustache. It was not a bit like Grandfather's friendly moustache, bushy and fair and turned up at the ends, but small, square and dark, making the man's face look rather stern.

A middle-aged stout lady with glasses rose from her desk at the front of the classroom.

'Heil Hitler, Frau Schweighofer!' she said in a piercing voice. 'And you must be Jutta. Come, I'll show you to your seat.'

I had to let go of Mama's hand and suddenly felt scared and very much alone among the thirty-odd boys and girls around me, all older and bigger than myself. Starting with the pupils at the back of the class the teacher then read out all our names and you had to jump up and shout: 'Present, Frau Hartmann!'

Then followed a song called *Deutschland, Deutschland, Über Alles*, which seemed to go on for a very long time. The tune was familiar but I didn't know the words, so I just copied the other children as they stood looking ahead with their right arms outstretched.

'Stand up straight and look at the Führer's picture!' the teacher barked at the girl next to me. Then:

'Erich, tell the new ones the name of our Führer!'

'Adolf Hitler, Frau Hartmam!' like the shot of a bullet came the reply from the back of the class.

'Now give me the Führer's salute!' commanded Frau Hartmann.

'Heil Hitler!' chanted the class, all jumping up with their right hands raised.

'That's how you greet everyone in the village and in your family,' we newcomers were told, 'and don't let me hear any more of that "Griesskoch" nonsense. Understood?'

We all nodded obediently but I did not get the joke. 'Grüss Gott!' did not sound vaguely like 'Griesskoch' (Semolina pudding) to me.

It was then that I noticed the spider sign on Frau Hartmann's necklace and ring. Only, it wasn't really a spider but something to do with the sun. The sun had been worshipped by our German forefathers, Frau Hartmann said, and the Swastika chosen by the Führer for the flag of the German Reich.

'Why is it black when everything round the sun is golden?' I wondered but dare not put my thoughts into words. While we sang about 'the black swastika in the white circle on the red flag' the teacher did not take her eyes off a small girl who kept fidgeting all through the song.

'I have to do a wee,' I could hear a scared little voice whisper. Lucky for Evi break-time was coming up. Nobody was to leave the classroom during lessons; Frau Hartmann had made that quite clear.

After break we got down to what was called 'serious work'. While the older pupils got on with their sums the teacher's attention was with the newest of her little flock. She chalked letters on the blackboard and we had to copy them onto our slates. When finally the i's, o's and a's met with her approval Frau Hartmam let us complete the line.

'Crash!' The noise of a pencil case dropped on the floor cut through the silence. Ears glowing, the owner dived under the bench to retrieve its contents. Some girls at the back started to giggle.

'Crash!' The teacher's cane coming down onto her desk made us all jump. 'Silence in class!' and immediately 30 small heads bowed over notebooks and slates and work was resumed.

What relief when at 11 o'clock my first schoolday had ended. Few mothers had come to collect their children. It was harvest time and with most men away in the war all hands were needed in the fields. But mine was there waiting and I dashed towards her. Then, suddenly, I remembered and for a moment stopped dead. Yet my right arm, dutifully raised, ended up in a tight hug around Mama.

'Heil Hitler!' wasn't right for greeting your mother, no matter what Frau Hartmann had said.

The night after my first schoolday was haunted by a horrible dream: The big, black spider had escaped from the flag and came crawling towards me . . . It began to entangle me in its sticky, grey web . . . Frozen in terror, I could not move, could not escape.

'Papa, help!' I cried out but Papa didn't hear me. He was far, far away in the war.

Frau Hartmann stood there but ignored me. She had eyes only for the man with the little moustache.

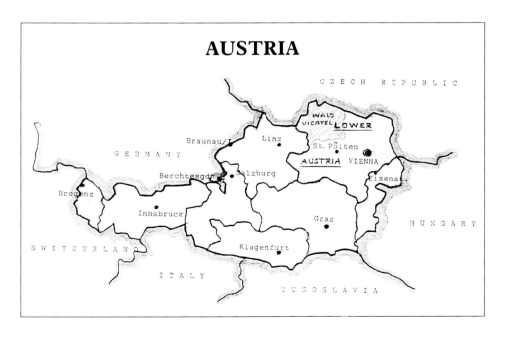

AUSTRIA

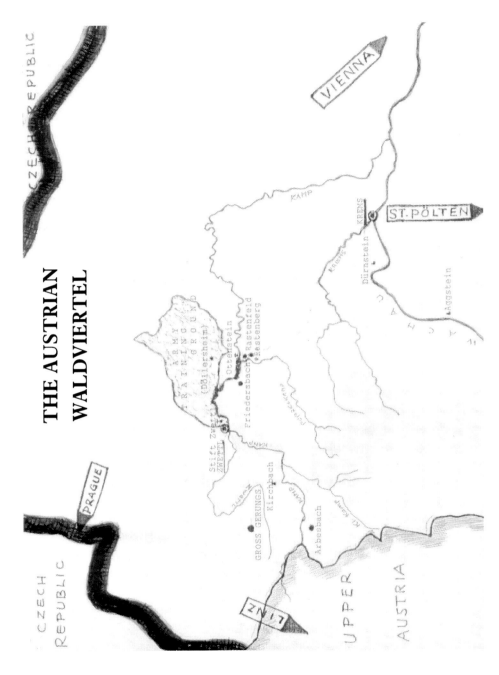

THE AUSTRIAN
WALDVIERTEL

CZECH REPUBLIC

VIENNA

ST. PÖLTEN

KREMS

KAMP

Dürnstein

Aggstein

ARMY
TRAINING
GROUND
(Döllersheim)

Ottenstein

Rastenfeld
Friedersbach Rastenberg

Stift Zwettl
ZWETTL

Kirchbach
GROSS GERUNGS

Arbesbach

PRAGUE

CZECH
REPUBLIC

ZN 7

UPPER

AUSTRIA

4

THE PRINCESS'S CASTLE

It was exactly a year ago that Papa went to war.

Again September sunshine lay over my home-village of Rastenfeld in the 'Waldviertel', the forest region of North-East Austria.

But the calm and brightness of the day contrasted sharply with the sombre mood gripping each member of my family as we said goodbye to dear Papa. A last hug and kiss and then the bus took him away to the war.

'Why does Papa have to be a soldier?' I asked my mum as we were left standing at the bus stop in the square. Mama didn't reply; she seemed preoccupied and miles away.

'Mama?' I kept tugging at her skirt but still no answer. How do you explain to a four-year-old that, with her homeland part of the German Reich, her father had to fight in the German army? When Mama bent down to pick me up her cheeks were wet with tears. I'd never seen my mother cry before – in my opinion grown-ups never cried – and started sobbing uncontrollably myself.

Back home my grandma popped a toffee into my mouth.

My home village, Rastenfeld.

Rastenfeld – church and school (behind tree).

Our house – 47 Market Square, Rastenfeld, Lower Austria.

'There, there, my sweety; don't you fret. You'll see, the war will be over very soon and Papa back home again.' But for once Omi had been quite wrong.

Our big house in the village square seemed strangely quiet and deserted. Of course, there was Mama, Omi, Opa and Hanni, the maid, not to mention Max, the Alsatian. But missing was someone very important indeed and would be for a long time to come.

After Papa's departure the family business was closed down. Some men came and took away the car and all the machines for making roof tiles and concrete pipes. 'Confiscated to help the war effort,' they said. I puzzled over what that could mean but regarded it as no great loss. Car journeys tended to make me sick, anyway and the disused builder's yard and empty outbuildings provided so much more space for playing!

There was only one forbidden area for me and my playmates, the lime-pit at the back of the yard.' I'd often watched from a safe distance as Papa's workmen made slaked lime. Water was pumped onto white stones in the pit causing a roar like a fire burning. A cloud of steam would rise and when it settled the lime-stones had turned into a white, creamy substance which would be used by the farmers for white-washing their cottages and stables.

'Don't you ever go near that lime-pit!' Papa had warned. 'If you touch the white stuff you'll be terribly burnt.' Nobody used the lime-pit any more and its wooden lid was firmly closed. But, all the same, the area remained taboo for us children.

When the cold weather stopped play outdoors I spent more and more time with my beloved grandma. Omi never tired of Ludo and Happy Families, she taught me all the long ballads and poems she knew by heart and her supply of wonderful stories never ceased. For me, climbing up the stairs to the granny flat came a close second to entering paradise.

My favourite haunt was Omi's living-room. Furnished with rustic pine, it was alive with colourful ornaments, plates, Toby-jugs and wood-carved farmers' heads. Its large bay window provided a view over the whole market square with St. Florian's fountain right in the centre. All through the summer it was surrounded by masses of scarlet geraniums. From wrought-iron boxes they would tumble down to where it said in fancy writing:

FRANZ TESCH and ERNST SCHWEIGHOFER
MASTER BUILDERS since 1908

Franz Tesch, my granddad, was now what Omi called retired, and Ernst Schweighofer, alias Papa, had to go to war and I missed him.

In winter I liked nothing better than curling up on the patchwork rug in front of the kachelofen (tiled stove) in Omi's lounge, enjoying the warmth of the crackling log fire, daydreaming, reading or listening to the cuckoo clock. Hand-carved in pine, it was crowned by a stag's head and had weights in the shape of fir cones, a wonderful combination of rustic craft and horological accuracy. How fascinating when the little door flew open and the cuckoo appeared, bowing and counting the hour. That from a very young age I could count and tell the time was all down to Omi's cuckoo clock.

My grandma's airy kitchen was at the back of the house. It overlooked the yard and the surrounding outbuildings and had access to a balcony. From there, secure behind wrought-iron railings, I loved to watch the birds or my own soap bubbles sail over the roofs into the world beyond. The area around the kitchen window was what we called Opa's 'no-go-zone'.

There, precariously perched on Omi's ironing-board, stood an elaborate castle, home to 'The Princess' – played by myself – and all her staff played by Omi. Constructed of building bricks it was quite fragile and earthquake-prone, hence the no-go-area for Opa.

Most of the time my granddad took the restrictions placed upon him with good humour. An outdoor type he normally limited his visits to the kitchen to meal-times. The rest of Opa's day was divided between his garden and his orchard. His fruit trees, grown from seed and carefully grafted, were his babies and he was justly proud of his crops of cherries, apples, pears and plums. There was always plenty of fruit for the family with the neighbours reaping the surplus. It took a lot of bad weather and persuasion from Omi for Opa not to be out in his darling orchard. Having to stay in the house always made him grumpy. Immediately he would start to complain about the Princess's castle.

'It's about time you moved that paraphernalia, my girl,' he'd grumble, 'and I want my armchair back now if you please.'

Why couldn't he see that his chair's velvet upholstery was the nearest thing to an Alpine meadow and essential grazing land for the royal livestock? But it was no good arguing when Opa was in that kind of mood. Luckily Omi nearly always sided with me and together we won the case. Armchair and ironing-board, it was decided, were allowed to stay for yet another day. Outvoted by the fairer sex once again, Opa would grab his newspaper and retire to the living-room. Through the half-open door we could hear him muttering something about 'petticoat government'.

The male-female imbalance in our house was temporarily redressed when Hami, the maid, left to get married and the Kurz family moved into the flatlet on the ground floor. Herr Kurz, a teacher at the local school, hardly lived up – or rather down – to his name which means 'Short' in German. A quiet man, he was tall and thin and sombre looking in his black suit. Herr Kurz was terrified of thunderstorms. At the first sign of a storm he would hide under the bedclothes and plead with his wife not to touch anything metal as this might cause lightning to strike. Frau Kurz was short with black, bobbed hair and a large bosom constantly heaving under a white pinafore.

'It's the woman who wears the trousers in that family,' I'd heard Mama say but I'd never seen Frau Kurz in trousers.

A disbeliever in sunshine and fresh air, Frau Kurz kept her sons indoors most of the time. I didn't care much for three-year-old Werner, a miserable whinging child. But baby Richard fascinated me as he sat in his pram, happily smiling through the wet-nappy-jungle of his mother's kitchen.

How dearly I would have loved a baby brother or sister of my own! But Mama did not share my enthusiasm.

'We can't have a baby while Papa is away in the war, dear.' What had the war got to do with it, I wondered. I thought long and hard and finally came up with the answer.

'Why don't we ask the Stork to bring a baby and surprise Papa when he comes home on leave?' It hurt that this serious and rather splendid suggestion met only with amusement on my family's side.

'Grown-ups can be strange at times,' I concluded and, sadly, I remained an only child.

I would have to make do with Ulli Brandtner from up the road. Her dad was also in the war and her mum had her hands full with the grocery shop and her baby daughter. To give Frau Brandtner a break Mama would take Ulli out most afternoons and for me it was the greatest honour to push her pram. Not having your own baby sister had one compensation: You could take her back to her mum when she cried.

My dear Omi with Mitzi – late 1940s.

THREE

THE LAND WITH THE
UNPRONOUNCEABLE NAME

The first letters Papa had sent from the war came from a strange place called Czechoslovakia.

'Cz-cho-va-kia? Where is that?' My tongue would never get round that peculiar name.

'It's the country across the border where Grandmother and Uncle Joschi come from,' Mama replied.

'Is that why they both speak so funny?' I wondered. Mama did her best to explain Grandmother's and Uncle Joschi's strange accents: 'You see, dear, in their younger days their homelands, like ours, belonged to one big country ruled by the Kaiser. German was spoken everywhere in that empire, although in a slightly different way.'

I then heard the story of my paternal grandmother, like most Bohemians a splendid cook, who as a girl had come to the Waldviertel to seek employment. How she had worked for a noble family until she met and married Grandfather, a young butcher and one of 24 (!) children. How they had scraped and toiled to advance from their tiny smallholding to a farm, an inn and a butcher's shop in Friedersbach, where they still lived. How Grandmother had opened a village post-office which she ran from a room next to the pub for many years. How business increased as bus passengers popped into the bar for a quick drink and 'Schweighofer' became a household name in the area. How Grandfather went to war and Grandmother was left in charge of the whole enterprise and three children, of whom Papa was the eldest.

'Your Friedersbach grandma is certainly an extraordinary lady,' Mama concluded.

Uncle Joschi's story was almost as fascinating.

Though not a real uncle like Papa's brothers, Karl and Willi, I regarded him as the next best thing. He always looked extremely handsome in his 'Steirer-Anzug', a grey, woollen suit with green oak-leaf trim and buttons made from stags' antlers. His 'Steirer-Hut', worn at a jaunty angle, was lifted every time my charming uncle greeted a lady.

Grandmother in the 1940s.   *Grandfather as I remember him.*

'Why does Uncle Joschi have a shaving brush stuck on his hat?' I once asked Papa. Being his friend he would know about such matters. Smiling, Papa explained that foresters used the 'Gamsbart' – made from the breast fur of the chamois – for decorative purposes and, to his knowledge, not for shaving.

From Papa I learned how Uncle Joschi came to be head forester to Count Thurn of Rastenberg. Born in a country called Silesia he'd come to Vienna to study at the university of Forestry and Agriculture. On completing his studies he found his homeland had become part of the newly created Czechoslovakia and decided not to return but to stay in Austria. With his new wife, a Viennese girl, he moved to the Waldviertel where he found employment at Count Thurn's estate. Before long he was in charge of the Count's extensive forests and responsible for both timber and game. Through buying all his building wood from Uncle Joschi he and Papa had become friendly.

I was pleased that my uncle had not gone back to the country with the unpronounceable name. Without him, life in the village would have been half the fun. Authorised by his employer, the Lord of the Manor, Uncle Joschi would always select the best trees from the Count's forests and have them delivered to Rastenfeld. Papa and his workmen would then perform the tricky task of erecting the decorated trees in the village square.

Thanks to Count Thurn, Uncle Joschi and Papa Rastenfeld kept winning prizes for the highest maypole and the most beautiful Christmas tree every year. I can still picture the scene as girls in dirndl dresses and boys in lederhosen danced round the maypole, weaving red and white ribbons into pretty patterns. And what a thrill to watch the most daring village lads climb the barkless trunk and retrieve chocolates and sausages from its very top! December would see the square transformed by a different magic, a giant Christmas tree.

No more Maypole dancing or carol singing under the big Christmas tree. Such irresponsible actions would attract enemy attention and such waste of resources could not to be tolerated in time of war.

Uncle Joschi's shooting parties, followed up by a feast of venison and wine were very popular with the farmers of Rastenfeld. But Papa took part in a deer hunt only once. The sight of the beautiful creature he'd just killed put him off shooting for life, he said. Aiming at people must have proved even more repulsive to my dad but, unfortunately, that's what wars seemed to be about.

Papa and his friend shared a great love of dogs. Uncle Joschi, an authority on the subject, had even written books on the breeding and training of hounds.

As much as I liked visiting the forester's cottage near the woods I was always in awe of the capercaillie in Uncle Joschi's hallway. With his stretched neck, open beak and wide-spread wings this huge game-bird looked most threatening to me. Creeping past him and all the other hunting trophies, I would head straight for the shed at the back. There, curled up with their mothers, were the loveliest puppies I'd ever seen. Immediately they would start fussing around me, licking my shoes and pulling my coat while Juno and Arne kept a watchful motherly eye on their offspring.

I was simply enchanted by Uncle Joschi's dog family and brown-and-white pointers featured quite heavily in my early paintings.

'I wish I had a dog,' I kept saying but Mama and Papa seemed to be deaf. Then, on my fourth birthday, 9 December, came the wonderful surprise: a black-and-tan Alsatian puppy with bright eyes and lovely soft ears.

I just stood there, wide-eyed and lost for words. Taking hold of my hand Papa put it on an oversized, clumsy front paw.

'Say hello to Max, your very own dog! He'll be your playmate and a guard dog for you all.' And, although only a youngster when Papa was drafted, an excellent guard dog he turned out to be. But boundless energy and a mischievous nature got Max into trouble many a time.

He seemed especially to have it in for Opa, forever hiding his slippers and pulling his Long Johns off the washing line. He also engaged in hunting trips which made him not too popular with foresters and farmers. And Opa didn't take kindly to broken windows and the large escape hole in the gate love-sick Max had created in pursuit of neighbours' lady dogs.

If Max wouldn't let me forget the day he joined the family I remembered

MY fifth birthday for different reasons. That morning I woke to a winter wonderland. The farm cottages peered sleepily from under white, fluffy bonnets and, just for my benefit, it seemed, Jack Frost had turned the village street into a sleigh run. But Mama didn't share my excitement. To coincide with my birthday she'd booked a photo session in the next town weeks before. But how could we now get to Zwettl, 15 kms from Rastenfeld, with the bus stuck in a snow drift and unlikely to resume its service? In the end Grandfather and his horses came to the rescue and saved the day.

'Fritz and Bruno can do with the exercise,' he grinned brushing the icicles from his bushy moustache. He wrapped me in a big, chequered blanket and lifted me onto the sleigh. Mama climbed aboard, too, and we were away.

Sandwiched between Grandfather and Mama I took in every detail of that enchanting journey: the tinkling of bells on the horses' harness, their

Me, aged five, in my first year at school (1939).

nodding heads and swishing tails as they trotted through woods full of glittering Christmas trees, and later, with their sleigh almost gliding on air, through a vast, snowy desert.

What happened at the Studio Lux after that magical sleigh ride I found rather boring. Yet my family seemed delighted with the result of the exercise, a dozen photos of me in different poses.

One, showing a serious, round-faced little girl looking up from a book, was declared overall favourite and duly sent off to Papa in the war.

Returning from Zwettl we broke the journey in Friedersbach where Grandmother was waiting with a warm welcome and a pot of hot stew.

The meal over, Grandfather gave me a conspiratorial wink. He lifted me onto a pub table and:

'The lion is loose, the lion is free,

He ripped apart his iron restraints . . .'

I began with great pathos and the usual slight lisp. *The Lion of Florence,* a ballad, Omi had taught me, was my favourite party piece.

The patrons' mouths gaped with amazement and their eyes nearly popped out of their heads as they followed my drama of a child rescued from a ferocious lion. Grandfather had watched my performance with great pride and a twinkle in his blue eyes. When he lifted me off the table I couldn't help wriggling and squirming. I never did like kisses from moustachioed men!

Then Uncle Karl brought in the birthday present for his small niece: a huge chocolate cake surrounded by five little candles and crowned by a big Mickey Mouse.

Like Papa, Uncle Karl was very artistic and could create fabulous novelty cakes. Walt Disney's magic had just reached the cinemas in our corner of the world and Mickey Mouse was everyone's favourite. For a while Uncle Karl's latest piece of culinary art enjoyed pride of place on the toy shelf. But finally my sweet tooth got the better of my preserving instincts and 'Birthday Mickey' didn't survive to see Christmas.

All through December the tantalising smells of Mama's baking had wafted through the house. Saint Nicholas had been and gone leaving fruit and nuts and gingerbread men and, opening the doors of the advent calendar, I kept counting the days until Christmas. At last the big moment had arrived. A tinkling silver bell announced the Christ Child's coming. The living-room door flew open and there stood the Christmas tree bathed in the light of a hundred candles. And oh, the wonderful presents! The sledge and the Wendy house and the doll with real hair who could close her eyes and say 'Mama!' Yet something very important was missing that Christmas Eve. Taking a celluloid angel from the top of the tree I carefully handed it to Mama.

'Will you send this to Papa in Cze-cho-va-kia, please? It's a guardian angel to look after him in the war . . .'

FOUR

A VERY SPECIAL GRANDMA

I'd often wondered about the stout lady with the pearl necklace and the smiling face whose picture Mama kept on her bedside table. The revelation came as a shock!

'This is my mother, darling, your real grandma. She died before you were even born.'

'B-b-ut I've got a grandma. Omi is my real grandma; she's got to be!' Confused and far too upset to listen to Mama's explanation I rushed upstairs and straight into Omi's arms.

'Mama says you aren't my real grandma, but you are, aren't you?'

My face buried in Omi's cardigan, I could no longer hold back the tears.

'Mama is right, sweetheart,' said Omi gently drying my eyes with her lacy handkerchief.

'Your real grandma was my best friend. We knew each other since our schooldays together. Our friendship continued when Rosa married your Opa and had a little girl, your mum.' So that's why Mama called Omi Tante (Auntie), not Mutter (Mother) as she should have done!

'Soon after Mama and Papa married,' Omi continued, 'your grandma fell very ill. We were all heartbroken when she died at only 46.' Omi reached for her hankie before she could talk again. 'I knew how lonely Opa was and we became very close. But when he finally asked me to marry him I had to think long and hard. I agreed under one condition: there had to be a baby in the house.

You see, I've always wanted a grandchild. My wish has been granted now I've got you.'

Well, that showed the matter in a totally different light. Heaving a deep sigh of relief I hugged my special grandma tightly.

'You were born in Vienna and I was the first one to see you,' she recalled. 'You were such a beautiful baby and, as a Sunday's child, a lucky one, too. When Mama asked me to be your godmother, I was thrilled to bits. A year later I married Opa and became your grandma; better still, don't you think?'

My first encounter with all the cousins, uncles and aunts I'd gained through Omi was through the photographs in her 'treasure' drawer. There were pictures of a youthful Omi in her Vienna office and many more of her walking, cycling or swimming, always surrounded by relatives and friends. I even spotted a very young Mama and Papa within the happy, exuberant crowd.

One very old photograph in Omi's collection caught my eye. It showed a family group, all very serious and formal.

'Who are these people with their funny clothes, hats and umbrellas?' I wanted to know.

'This is me at the age you are now with my four brothers and sisters,' Omi explained. 'We are all wearing our Sunday best. And these aren't

My parents on their wedding day (1 January 1933).

Omi in 1935, the year she married my granddad.

Opa at the time of his second marriage (October 1935).

umbrellas but parasols, dear. In my younger days all ladies wore hats and carried parasols to protect their skin from the sun.'

How strange. I'd always been told that pale was unhealthy. That's why Mama insisted I'd play out in the sun. The few people I knew wearing hats nowadays did so for quite different reasons.

Omi for instance had very sensitive eyes and Opa's bald head was susceptible to all kinds of weather. And, of course, most ladies wore hats in church, especially at weddings and funerals.

'This is my elder brother to whom I was closest of all,' Omi cut short my reflections on the wearing of hats. 'He was called Franz after our dad and so was his only son.'

While counting up all the Franzes in Omi's life, including Opa, I saw a sudden sadness overshadow her face.

'Both, Franz and my younger brother, Emil, shown here next to me, died an early, tragic death. And it's unlikely I'll see Franz junior ever again. He and his wife fled to England some years ago.'

'But, Omi, why did your brothers die and your nephew go to a foreign country?'

Omi (front) as a five-year-old with her brothers and sisters.

'You are far too young to understand such tragedies, darling. I'll explain when you are a little bit older.'

'I haven't seen Martha for a great many years,' Omi pointed to one of her sisters on the photograph, 'She and her family live in South Tyrol which belongs to Italy since the last war. You see, dear, crossing borders is not very easy these days.'

Contemplating the fate of some members of my extended family my mind was made up: never would I go to a country with a strange foreign language and a border you weren't allowed to cross.

At least great-aunt Josephine, Omi's other sister, had stayed in Vienna. Her daughters Herta and Luise and their children were frequent visitors here.

But out of my four Viennese cousins I only liked Lieselotte. Gerhard, in my eyes, was a big know-all and Dieter and Helmut were just silly boys. I never forgot the embarrassing moment when they'd once fought over me. In the end they'd reached the decision, that they would both marry me. I was never asked but at four-and-a-half had no desire to marry, least of all Dieter and Helmut.

Another very interesting picture in Omi's drawer was that of a beautiful lady in an elaborate gown. Dark plaited hair interwoven with white, starry flowers surrounded her lovely face like a crown.

'This is the Empress Elisabeth, or Sissi as she was known,' Omi pointed out. 'Her husband, Kaiser Franz Josef, reigned over the big empire which was lost after the last war.'

'D'you mean the war which made Grandmother and Uncle Joschi Czech and your sister Italian, Omi?'

'The very same, darling. Wars always bring tragedy and upheaval to a great many people. Let's hope this one won't turn out quite as bad.'

Returning to the portrait of the beautiful Sissi Omi's mood lightened again.

'You won't believe this, but I nearly became the empress's goddaughter,' she smiled. 'You see, every girl born on Christmas Eve, the empress's birthday, was entitled to that. But my dad couldn't face all the fuss that came with the honour. So he falsely registered my birth as December 23rd.'

My face glowed with pride. Who else could boast a grandma with an empress as her rightful godmother! That added yet another jewel to Omi's crown. But then I had known all along that mine was the most special, most wonderful grandmother in the entire world!

Omi was very religious. She taught me prayers and hymns and would take me to church the odd Sunday if I promised to sit still. Omi had a 'Great Book of Saints' with gold leaf and many pictures in it and its stories made fascinating reading. My favourite was St. Nicholas, who returned to earth every 6th of December to hand out treats for good children. I also liked St. Francis, who was so fond of animals he could talk to them in their own language. And was I pleased for St. Elisabeth, when she escaped punishment from her mean, cruel husband, as the food she had brought for the poor miraculously turned into roses. But I had my doubts about St. Martin. Charitable and well meaning he might have been, but to me he lacked common-sense. Why cut your coat and give half to the beggar? Half a coat was no good to anyone, especially the part with no sleeves in!

As Omi pointed out, the saints played an important role in country life. Every village had its own patron saint whose statue held a prominent position. St. Florian, a Roman soldier, was watching over Rastenfeld's homes, barns and stables. As the fire-fighters' patron saint, he made sure they didn't burn down when struck by lightning. My Friedersbach grandparents must have felt very safe having the statue of Our Lady right in front of their inn. St. Mary also happened to be the patron of Friedersbach church.

'Before the war we always had big celebrations on the feast day of the church patron saint,' Omi would reminisce. 'People came from all over the Waldviertel to join such 'Kirtag' festivities. There was eating, drinking and dancing from morning till night and both, young and old, enjoyed the many stalls, carousels and various other rides. Farm-lads would buy gingerbread hearts with sentimental rhymes for their sweethearts and many a business deal or, indeed, marriage proposal was made on such a day. 'Kirtag in Friedersbach was always popular because of your grandfather's famous wines and your grandmother's excellent cooking.'

Pity, I wasn't old enough to remember those festivities. We still had Corpus Christi celebrations, but they were purely religious. Accompanied by altar boys, flower girls, the band and a large congregation, the parish priest would carry the monstrance round the village square. He would pause at four special altars for a blessing preceded by hymns and long prayers in Latin. It was a great honour to be a flower girl at the Corpus Christi procession. Wearing a white dress and flowers in your hair you scattered rose petals on the path of the Holy Sacrament or you held on to one of four ribbons attached to a silk cushion. Balancing the statues of saints on those cushions was a tricky business and therefore reserved for older girls.

The Auferstehung celebrations at Easter followed a similar pattern. A statue of the risen Christ was carried in triumph to the church.

Not only parishes but every parishioner had his or her personal saint. And to the farmers their 'Namenstag', the day of the saint they were named after, was more important than their birthday. People congratulating the celebrant on 'Namenstag' would always be treated to wine or coffee and cakes.

It was beyond me how Vroni Fessl, unable to read or write, could memorise every villager's saint's day while the rest of us had to look them up in the calendar.

Some of the names in there made me giggle. Wouldn't you just love to be called 'Philomena', 'Eulalia' or 'Maud'! Mind you, I wasn't too keen on my own name, listed on 22 December.

'The name "Jutta" was your mum's choice,' Omi informed me, 'old German names were in when you were born. But, thinking back to your christening, it didn't go down too well with the old priest. So, to keep everyone happy, we added "Maria" as your middle name. You can't get any more saintly than Our Lady, now can you? Besides, "Maria" gives a pleasant, melodious ring to a severe name like "Jutta", don't you think?'

Clever Omi! Of course, I agreed.

To me Omi was a saint herself. Who would have thought that for a long time she had remained outside the church? As she confessed to me years later, it was all because of the heartache over her brothers. Unable to cope with marital problems, Franz had committed suicide and consequently been refused a Christian funeral. And Emil, excommunicated for choosing cremation rather than a burial, had suffered the same fate when he met an untimely death. In defiance, their grieving sister had turned her back on the Catholic church whose strict dogma she could no longer accept. It was only at the time of my christening that Omi had returned to the flock.

FIVE

WHERE THE LORD RESTED

I hardly recognised our parish priest when, without his church robes, he arrived for the first R.E. lesson at school. He explained mass with the help of pop-up cardboard pictures and told us stories about Jesus, the apostles and the saints. But R.E. appeared most boring for the older pupils who had to struggle with long-winded questions from the catechism. One subject seemed to be very close to Pfarrer Ledl's heart:

'Hands up who went to mass on Sunday!' was his first address on Monday morning. Then, one by one, those pupils with their hands down were interrogated about their absence from church.

'I had nothing to wear, Herr Pfarrer,' served as the favourite excuse, especially after clothes rationing had started. For school you could turn up in clogs, wellingtons or even bare-foot, but everyone dressed up for church.

But R.E. played only a minor part in the schools of the Third Reich and our class teacher made sure we got our priorities right.

Frau Hartmann was Adolf Hitler's number one fan and hardly a lesson went by when his name wasn't mentioned. We heard about the great man's early years in the border town of Braunau ('What a privilege to be born in the same country as the Führer!'), his immense artistic talent, his unmatched bravery in the fight for his country and his struggle to make Germany a better place for all German people.

We learned that Adolf Hitler's roots were only a short distance from our home village ('The Führer even sacrificed his grandmother's grave in Döllerheim together with the village and its surroundings for a vital army training ground. But, you never know, one day he might return to the area and honour us with his visit.')

Each schoolday would start with five verses each of *Deutschland, Deutschland Über Alles* and *Die Fahne Hoch!* – and God help you if your arm got tired and sank below the required height!

Frau Hartmann's favourite topic was the Führer's love for his German boys and girls and what was expected of us to be worthy of this privilege. Discipline and physical fitness were immensely important and competitive games and races the best way to achieve this aim. Lacking the 'healthy fighting spirit' demanded by Frau Hartmann and the Führer I never enjoyed such activities as much as I should have done. And, considering what lay ahead of us in the Hitler Youth – or in my case, the B.D.M. (League of German Maidens) – I was not exactly looking forward to the age of ten. At that time nobody thought it possible for the 'Reich of a Thousand Years' to have collapsed by 1945.

If I wasn't too keen on outdoor games I definitely hated P.E. in class. Overcoming the lack of proper apparatus, Frau Hartmann had devised obstacle races over desks and benches and break-neck exercises on the blackboard stand. And, timid by nature, I would fail miserably in most of them. How I envied and admired Erna Reiter who climbed like a monkey and won every single race. That she wasn't over-endowed with grey matter seemed quite irrelevant to me.

However, my hero-worship of Erna ended abruptly on the day she turned blackmailer and cheat.

'I'll tell the teacher!' she had threatened gloating over the embarrassing puddle under my seat, 'But then I might not if you promise to do my homework for me every day.' I promised but lived in constant fear Frau Hartmann might detect one or the other of my 'crimes' and punish me accordingly. My salvation came in the unlikely blessing of measles and tonsillitis. Not even the massive doses of cod-liver-oil, called 'Fischerl-Honig' (Fish honey) by Mama, could spoil my enjoyment of that bout of ill health.

Returning to school after several weeks' absence I found that the blackmail had stopped. Unfortunately, another peril was looming in the person of needlework teacher Lydia Glatz. She didn't have a bald head as her name suggested but wore her hair in a bun. A middle-aged spinster like Frau Hartmann, she was much thinner and even fiercer.

Our first needlework project looked fun. What sense of achievement when, after hours of weaving, my self-produced skipping rope poked through the cotton-reel hole. But learning to crochet was harder and knitting more difficult still. Patience was not one of Frau Glatz's virtues. A dropped stitch could make her fly into a rage, and to punish our 'useless fingers' she would liberally apply the cane.

I was luckier than most of my class-mates as Omi, herself a trained needlework teacher, could help me with tricky homework set by Frau Glatz. Even so she inevitably found fault with the thumbs of my mittens and the heels of my socks. How I dreaded those needlework lessons. I almost envied the boys for their extra P.E. during the time we had to suffer Frau Glatz.

What relief when the school doors closed for the weekend and another 'Friedersbach-Day' was in sight. Most Sundays, weather permitting, Mama and I spent with Papa's parents in Friedersbach. It would take my little legs some one-and-a-half hours to walk the six kilometres to the next village but it wasn't so much my legs that tired, rather my brain because of the wretched times-tables drill. However, in fairness to Mama, that only happened when illness had made me fall behind with my sums.

The road to Friedersbach followed the Purzelkamp as it tumbled and gushed through a wooded valley (*purzeln* = tumble). Mama explained how the fast flowing water had shaped and polished the stones in the river to make them look like ostrich or even dinosaur eggs. Steep rocks, piled up like a giant's building bricks, formed a sheer wall along one side of the valley. Up and up they went until they almost reached the sky. According to Frau Hartmann the Waldviertel's strange rock formations were relics of ice-age mountains crumbling away in the course of time but I wasn't satisfied with this explanation. Didn't names like 'Pilzstein' (Mushroom Rock), 'Wackelstein' (Wobble Rock) and 'Teufelsbett' (Bed of the Devil) suggest otherwise? Following your own imagination you could always add to the sagas folklore had spun around those peculiar stones. My declared favourite was the *Herrgottstein* (Rock of Our Lord). The half-way mark of our journey, it always made a welcome resting place.

'Please, Mama, lift me up!' I'd pester as soon as the massive stone came in sight. Astride the moss-covered boulder I'd feel the familiar large footprint and poke my finger into the hole clearly created by a walking-stick. And I'd beg Mama again to tell the story of how Rastenfeld received its name.

'A long, long time ago,' she'd start, 'Jesus was walking across the

A field of flowering poppies, near Friedersbach.

My grandparents' inn in Friedersbach.

Waldviertel which in those days was nothing but a wilderness. Tired and thirsty, he decided to rest on a big stone next to a river. Many years later settlers came to the area and discovered the stone with Our Lord's footprint. They cleared the forest and built a village nearby which they named 'Rastenfeld' (Rest in the Field).' I loved this saga and was immensely proud of my home village's claim to fame. What other place in the world could trace its origin to a site chosen by Jesus himself? And if Jesus didn't have divine taste, who did?

The valley of the Purzelkamp offered just about anything town people came to look for in the country:

In spring its forests were carpeted with snow-drops, primroses and forget-me-nots. In summer wild strawberries, raspberries, brambles and mushrooms were there for the picking. And wildlife in abundance could be enjoyed throughout the seasons: trout leaping in the Kamp's clear, chilly waters, playful hares doubling and somersaulting by its banks and bushy-tailed squirrels nibbling the fruits of the forest. You could hear woodpeckers hammering on tree trunks and spot groups of deer happily grazing in the clearings. It was an oasis of peace. Who could have guessed that not so far from here a ferocious war was raging?

Leaving the shade of the forest behind the valley would open into a patchwork of fields and on the hill in the distance we could see Friedersbach church. My steps would suddenly quicken as from there it was only minutes to the welcoming inn under the chestnut trees.

The throaty bark of Barry, the giant St. Bernard, would greet you, you'd be encased in Grandmother's arms and endure Grandfather's tickly kiss. A hearty meal would be waiting and you could drink as much lemonade as you wished.

While Mama helped with the dishes you'd enjoy the guided tour through the Schweighofer's realm led by Grandfather and Barry. You'd cuddle the cats, feed the hens and visit the cows, pigs and horses.

When the bar wasn't busy Uncle Karl might harness Fritz and Bruno and give you a ride in the Landau, and if you were specially lucky you'd even catch Willi at home.

Willi was Papa's youngest brother and when he wasn't at college he was usually at camp; not a holiday camp, far from it. They were made to work very hard there, cutting down trees and building new roads, Willi said. Like the unemployed, all school-leavers had to partake in this Reichsarbeitsdienst (National Labour Service), I heard.

With an 18 years' gap between Papa and Willi my uncle was closer to my generation and I simply adored him.

'Please, drop the "uncle", Jutta, you make me feel really old,' he'd insist and I'd blush and oblige. Who would mind losing an uncle when gaining such a wonderful friend!

Willi was going to be a teacher and could do simply anything. He played the piano, accordion, violin and guitar, was brilliant at drawing and painting and equally gifted for sports.

'If only I had a teacher like Willi,' I kept thinking as his long, slender fingers made birds, piglets and dogs from the cankers and fir cones weld gathered together. For Willi I'd do anything, even sit still for an hour. That's how long it normally took him to draw a portrait of me. Willi was also Papa's declared favourite. Not once had he missed his kid brother's bus when it passed through Rastenfeld at the beginning of term.

'Here's a little extra for a poor student,' he'd say and slip one or two notes into Willi's pocket. Papa knew from his own student days how hard it could be to make ends meet in a city.

But then came the day when Papa himself had to leave from that bus stop but not for St. Pölten, much further, for war . . .

SIX

THE POLISH CORRIDOR

I always admired the ingenious way farmers balanced sacks of potatoes, firewood and their small children on wooden push-carts and was desperate to call such a marvellous means of transport my own.

'Forget it, Jutta! You've got a doll's pram. What on earth do you want a push-cart for?' Mama sometimes despaired over my peculiar requests. But if she wouldn't listen, perhaps the Easter Bunny would! Going by the amount of snow still around in April 1941 one wouldn't have guessed that Holy Week was upon us already. The frost had held back the catkins of the Pussy Willow, so there wouldn't be many 'palms' to be blessed during Palm Sunday's mass.

What, if flying to Rome on Maundy Thursday the church bells lost their way in the snow clouds? The excitement of announcing Holy Week services with football rattles would soon wear off with the altar boys. However, church bells must have excellent homing instincts; on Holy Saturday they had safely returned, joyfully tolling over the rising of Christ.

During the long Latin mass on Easter Sunday my mind kept wandering to the profane side of the feast. Waste of time, looking for eggs in the garden this year . . . Easter Bunny would have given up delivering as a bad job.

'Perhaps you should try places more sheltered,' Mama suggested.

Following her advice and the string of paw marks running along the outside of the yard I arrived at the covered drive-way. And there, surrounded by Easter eggs, stood my dream come true, a child-sized push-cart. A note attached to it read:

'Durch Eis und Schnee musst' ich heut fahren
zu dir mit diesem netten Karren.
Dafür musst du mir fleissig essen
und auch aufs Folgen nicht vergessen.'

(I had to come through ice and snow
to deliver this handsome push-cart for you.
In return you must try and eat better
and never be disobedient.)

Asking Mama to read me the verse again and again I came to the conclusion the last line was added for rhyming's sake only. I always – well, nearly always – did as I was told, didn't I?

However, when it came to the bit about eating, the Easter Bunny did have a point. Since starting school I'd caught everything going: tonsillitis, measles, chicken-pox and, worst of all, whooping cough. There'd been only one good thing about this terrible illness, being allowed to sleep in Mama's big double bed and held and comforted during the horrible nightly attacks.

The whooping cough had ruined my appetite and left me pale, weak and skinny. I couldn't even look at Opa's cabbage, spinach and lettuce and Mama had become very concerned.

But to catch me dropping best stewing steak under the table for Max had made her furious.

'Town people would give anything for meat like this,' she'd scolded, 'and you are wasting it on the dog!'

Perhaps Mama was right and so was the Easter Bunny. From now on I would make an effort and eat all my meat and greens.

There was still plenty to eat in the country but food rationing had hit our towns. Many Viennese came to the Waldviertel to exchange clothes, jewellery, furniture and carpets for potatoes, butter and eggs, an activity we called 'Hamstern'. The bomb scare over German cities made many more move to rural areas where they felt safe.

That's how Omi's niece, Herta and her children, Lieselotte and Gerhard, came to live in Rastenfeld. Their dad, Omi told me, was detained in Persia where he had gone to build bridges and tunnels before the war.

I soon became friends with Lotte, two years younger and even skinnier than I, but I couldn't stand 13-year-old Gerhard, who always talked down to his sister and me.

'You don't really believe that the Stork delivers babies and a hare brings the Easter eggs?' he'd snigger and: 'There is no such thing as fairies in the garden.' But Lotte and I knew better and didn't let Gerhard spoil our wonder-world.

A stool with our best dolls' china would be set for the fairies every evening and the following morning all the pretend-food had gone. If that wasn't proof of the fairies' existence, what was? Of course, we never suspected Opa to be playing the role of Fairy King!

Although she was a good friend, Lotte once got me into trouble.

'I bet you can't jump over that lake in the yard,' she dared me one rainy morning. Accepting the challenge I took a big leap and – landed right in the middle. Max, trying to rescue me from the puddle, got hold of my coat and – something ripped.

Wet through with a tear in my coat I had to face Mama. As expected she was very cross.

'Just look at the state of your clothes!' she shouted. 'You'd better look after your things, my girl. There is a war on, you know.' As if I needed reminding! The war seemed to stop all the fun.

'The Führer never wanted to fight Britain and France. It was they who interfered and started the war,' Frau Hartmann had told the older pupils, 'And it was all over the Polish Corridor.'

She went on about German territorial rights in Poland but I wasn't really listening any more.

Fancy starting a war over a silly corridor! And how could so many Poles fit into a corridor in the first place? It just didn't make sense. I would have to ask Nina; perhaps she could explain. Nina was Grandmother's new maid who had come all the way from Poland to help in the kitchen and on the farm. I liked Nina a lot. She had thick plaited hair, splendid teeth and a lovely smile. And when she wasn't singing Polish songs she was chewing sunflower seeds. It fascinated me how Nina could store the husks in one corner of her mouth to finally spit them out in squirrel fashion. I could never, ever match this skill, no matter how desperately I tried. Attempting to correct my technique Nina would pull funny faces and in the end we'd both collapse with the giggles.

Nina was fun to be with but her command of German wasn't that great. That's why our conversation never did stretch as far as the Polish Corridor.

It was with the news of Papa's posting to Danzig that the Polish question came into focus again.

'What's Papa doing in Nina's country?' I was curious to know. 'Papa is making sure that the Polish Corridor, that is the German part near Danzig, is staying German from now on, dear.'

Mama had clarified the mystery of the corridor but the question of war over Poland still bothered me. How could anyone regard Nina and the other young Poles who worked so hard for our farmers as the enemy?

There was no doubt in my mind, however, on which side the British stood. Firstly, they'd started the silly war and now they were sending their planes to drop bombs on our cities.

'Hell-bent on destroying our industry, they don't care about killing women and children in their air-raids night and day,' Frau Hartmann kept ranting, 'and people are stupid and treacherous enough to listen to the *Schwarzsender* (enemy broadcast) and believe all the lies they hear.'

In no uncertain terms we were told of our duty to report such 'traitors' or indeed anyone who made disparaging remarks against the Führer and his noble cause.

'It is the greatest honour for every German to defend the Reich against enemy aggression or even die for our beloved fatherland,' was Frau Hartmann's comment as more and more of our men were drafted into military service.

My grandparents' reaction was very different when the Führer called upon their second son.

'Maybe Uncle Karl and Papa could visit each other in Poland?' I tried to comfort Grandmother, but to no avail.

'Not likely, dear. Poland is a big country,' she sighed, rubbing her eyes until they were really red. It was then that I realised how much I had underestimated that wretched corridor.

The next one to be drafted was Sepp Gutmam, the village carpenter, married to Hanni, our former maid. Then, despite Count Thurn's objections, the war machine caught up with most of his employees.

'What will happen to Arne and Juno and the pups when Uncle Joschi has to go to war?' I fretted.

'I'm sure the dogs are the least of Auntie Milli's problems,' Mama said. 'The poor dear has to leave the forester's house and go back to Vienna to live with her family.'

Herr Kurz's call to the colours meant the reduction of our school from three classes to two. And Frau Hartmann became even stricter having to cope with many more pupils in her care. I wasn't too bothered about my teacher's problems; my concern was over Herr Kurz. How would the poor man, so afraid of thunderstorms, react to all the shooting of the war?

Our school became really overcrowded as more and more children from the industrial Ruhr were evacuated to the south of the Reich.

'A girl from Essen will be staying with us for a while,' Mama announced one day.

'She might eat a lot coming from a place like that (*Essen* = eat),' was my first reaction, thinking of my own poor appetite. Resi did turn out a big eater, devouring everything on her plate with lightning speed, but her table manners, I noticed, left much to be desired. Her other bad habits were spitting, swearing and wetting the bed but Mama never punished her as she would have certainly done me.

'Resi has been through a lot what with air-raids and family trouble,' Mama explained. 'We must try to be kind and patient with the poor mite.' But there was a limit to my tolerance and patience as Resi turned really nasty towards me. Not only did she tell lies to my school-friends, Mama and Omi, she pushed in the eyes of my doll and drew rude pictures in my exercise book. What a relief when, several months later, a clean, healthy looking Resi joined the children's transport back to the Ruhr.

'You won't believe this,' Mama said, reading the thank-you-letter from Resi's mother. 'The silly girl left the case with all her new clothes and toys behind on the train.'

There was one way of telling German evacuees from the local schoolboys before they even opened their mouths: They all had crew-cuts, some even sported shaved heads. Frau Hartmann was all in favour of that kind of hairstyle as it helped in the fight against lice. Most girls in our class wore plaits – Frau Hartmann called them 'louse-ladders' – but Mama insisted that my hair was kept short. Yet, much to everybody's horror, I still managed to catch lice at school.

'There's only one answer to the problem,' Omi remarked, 'a good drenching with paraffin.' (Paraffin lamps were always on stand-by in case blizzards should cause power-cuts.) I shall never forget the experience: soaked with this foul smelling liquid my hair, wrapped in towels, was left to 'stew' overnight. And then it took several shampoos and camomile rinses to get rid of the awful paraffin stench.

Mama and Omi swore by camomile tea. Not only did it cure tummy troubles, it also kept my hair blonde.

SEVEN

POPPIES AND CLOGS AND BABIES CALLED ADOLF

Mama made sure I was always turned out well. She created my numerous 'designer' jumpers and hats from various bits of left-over wool. Mama was an excellent knitter but sewing, she said, wasn't her cup of tea. Since her eyes had got worse, Omi, too, had to give up needlework but we could always fall back on Frau Österreicher, our dressmaker friend. I sometimes wondered why the Führer hadn't changed Österreichers' name when he made Österreich (Austria) the Ostmark of the German Reich. 'Ostmärker' would have sounded so much better than an old-fashioned name like 'Österreicher', I thought.

The friendship between our two families went back a very long time.

It was the Österreichers Opa bought this house from when he first came to Rastenfeld,' Mama informed me, 'and that's what it looked like back in 1908. The building on the old picture postcard was nothing like our present house.

'Opa made many improvements to the original farm, house,' Mama explained, 'and the first-floor extension is all Papa's work. That part was only added in 1935 when Opa and Omi married.'

'After selling their house the Österreicher family moved across the road,' Mama continued, 'and Anni and I used to play together when we were little girls.'

Anni was Österreichers' unmarried daughter, whom I liked very much.

She ran the smallholding with her father, the village barber, who was also responsible for cutting any hair. I hardly knew their son, Rudi, who, like Papa, had been a soldier since the start of the war.

I'd never ever seen Frau Österreicher leave the house. Her flat feet in flat carpet slippers seemed to be rooted to the pedal of her sewing-machine. Frau Österreicher could perform miracles on that old rattle-trap, turning Mama's worn coats and dresses into new ones for me. But she would not take money for her dressmaking skills, so Mama offered to help with the harvest. This seemed a fair exchange for both parties concerned. There were no mod-cons at Österreichers' farm and everything was down to hard labour. I can still hear Anni's and her father's razor-sharp scythes swish through the meadows in an unchanging rhythm. In their wake Mama and

I would rake the grass into neat heaps. They had to be turned again and again with wooden pitch forks until the hay was dry and ready for loading. In the absence of proper horse-power two long-suffering cows pulled the cart. As for me, riding home on top of Österreichers' hay-wagon always meant being on top of the world.

'Cows are musical creatures,' Anni would say, urging me to sing to them at milking time. Of course, it was I who took all the credit for Lisa's and Greta's increased milk yield. At Anni's request I would climb the steep ladder to the hay-loft and search for eggs some crafty hen might have hidden where grown-ups just couldn't get. But it was the bread-baking ceremony which beat all the other events on Österreichers' farm.

With the baker away in the war the farmers had reverted back to their old skills. And home-grown rye, ground at the water-mill down the road, produced the most delicious crusty bread which kept fresh for weeks. Österreichers' bread-baking ceremony always stretched over two days. Firstly, the dough would be mixed, kneaded and put into flat wicker moulds to 'prove' overnight. By the morning the fire in the brick-built bread oven had burnt out and, fascinated, I would watch Anni push the risen loaves into its glowing mouth. So that's how Hansl and Gretl must have got rid of the wicked witch! A delicious by-product of Österreichers' bread-baking ceremony were pancake look-a-likes called '*Flecken*'. Made to their own recipe they tasted best straight from the oven spread with butter or cream.

New potatoes, roasted on open fires after a busy day in the fields, were another culinary feast. But reaping the Waldviertel's most lucrative crop meant extremely hard, back-breaking work for both diggers and pickers. By comparison, the poppy harvest was pure pleasure. Poppies looked pretty at any time of the year. In spring delicate pink and white flowers would splash colour all over the stark Waldviertel landscape. Their petals shed, tiny green seed heads would appear, each topped with a delicate crown. By August, having grown bigger and woody, the capsules were ready for picking.

'Poppies can harm you,' Mama warned once or twice, watching me empty one pod after another straight into my mouth. But, like the empty shells, my mother's words were thrown to the wind. Surely, a delicious product, so frequently used in farmhouse cooking, could only be good for you! Then one day Anni told me the sad story of Freddy and Vroni Fessl: Fed an extract of green poppy heads the Fessl babies would be kept asleep for most of the day while their ignorant parents were busy at work.

'And look, what's happened to the pair later in life,' Ami concluded. As every villager knew, Freddy and Vroni, now middle-aged, were seriously retarded. Unable to look after themselves, they were kept in the local workhouse, the responsibility of the council. The sad tale of Freddy and Vroni completely changed my mind about the unlimited benefits of poppies.

Like Anni Österreicher, most farmers in our village wore clogs instead of shoes and so did their children. How I envied my class-mates for their versatile, hard wearing footwear! Clogs were ideal for sliding down planks and skating on ice, and your one pair of precious shoes could be saved for best. My Viennese cousin, Lotte, also regarded clogs as the best thing on earth. We pestered and pestered until our mums finally relented and took us to Kesslers to have our feet measured. Herr Kessler was the best clogmaker in Rastenfeld. He also dug graves but preferred being called 'funeral director'. Arriving at the cottage next to the cemetery, Lotte and I were a bit scared of the withered little man with the croaky voice who smelled of tobacco and leather. But the result of our visit was brilliant: the most handsome clogs with carved wooden soles and stitched leather uppers.

I could never understand why Mama wouldn't let me wear my precious new footwear for school. Neither, it seemed, could Frau Kessler, the clogmaker's battle-axe spouse. Every first Monday of the month she would come strutting towards our house, clogs on her feet and washboard under her arm.

'Can't stand gossiping. Must get on with my work!' she'd say, clatter down the steps to the wash-house and disappear in a thick cloud of steam. She'd make up for it though when re-emerging with a huge wicker basket full of gleaming white washing.

'Here, give us a hand with t' pegs as you ain't doing naught anyroad!' I would be greeted the moment I'd get home from school. Frau Kessler didn't care much for children or pets and she truly hated Max.

'Dogs what rip t' washing off t' line are fit for naught but putting down!' she would mutter and I made sure Max was kept out of mischief and Frau Kessler's sight.

As the washerwoman to several households in Rastenfeld Frau Kessler was well up on local news. And she made sure gossip spread quickly among all her clients in Rastenfeld.

I remember one washday when Hilda Braun was the object of Frau Kessler's disapproval.

'Did you know that daft lass had another kid?' Mama was told over lunch. (She didn't).

'That's her third brat now and none has a father. Shouldn't be allowed that sort of carry-on if you ask me.' Nobody had asked her but Frau Kessler continued all the same.

'And guess what she's called it. Why, Adolf of course!'

Whenever babies were mentioned I immediately pricked up my ears. Rastenfeld now boasted a few little Adolfs. The Führer would be pleased about that. He seemed so very fond of children; I'd seen pictures of him holding babies with boys and, girls crowding around. The Führer could perform miracles, Frau Hartmann had said. Perhaps I should ask him for a baby brother or sister? But perhaps not.

The man who sent Papa to war and made Willi dig roads could hardly be trusted with a problem like mine. Despite Gerhard's mockery I decided I'd rather stick with the Stork.

EIGHT

LA BICYCLETTE

I was fed up with having to be quiet when the news was on. It always seemed to be over one thing, the Wehrmacht's spectacular successes on the Western Front.

At school it was just the same. Frau Hartmann never stopped talking about our troops' triumphant march into Paris and the humiliating French surrender.

'After the last war,' she explained, 'France stole from us a large area along the Rhine and by denying us "essential breathing space" tried to wipe out the German nation.'

Her eyes shining behind her horn-rimmed spectacles, she would proclaim with passion:

'It was the greatest moment for the Führer and the entire Reich to see justice done and have that territory back in German hands.'

For me, only one event after Papa's posting to French Alsace-Lorraine was all important. An enormous wooden crate addressed to 'Fräulein Jutta Schweighofer' had arrived at our house one day. With a mounting sense of excitement I'd watched the locksmith assemble its intriguing contents. The end result: a miniature bike, the exact replica of a lady's bicycle, complete with bell, reflectors and a fancy lemon-and-white safety net over the back wheel. I was bowled over!

My French bicycle made me the envy of all my school friends, especially once I had mastered the dream machine. In the absence of stabilisers this wasn't easy but I was determined to ride my bike by the time Papa came home on leave. The first practice runs took place in our yard with me pedalling frantically to stay upright and Mama running along holding on to the saddle. Once I had found my balance, she occasionally let go while I, unaware of the divorce, carried on. Unfortunately, the plank around Opa's vegetable patch kept getting in the way and I'd end up, head first, in the cabbage bed. After some weeks of permanently scraped and iodine painted elbows and knees the moment of triumph had arrived: Mama thought me competent enough to venture onto the village green. But I had to wait several more months before I could show off my new skill to Papa.

My bike proved a big asset on the Sunday trips to Friedersbach and, with a tremendous final spurt, I always arrived there ahead of Mama. Normally, my two small cousins would be on the lookout for me.

'Please, please, let me have a go on your bike!' Rolf would pester, followed by little Kurt's echo: 'Me too, me too!' But their mum, my Auntie Rosi, wouldn't hear of it.

'You two aren't big enough for cycling,' she'd warn them. 'I don't want you to break your necks or that lovely bike of Jutta's, d'you hear?'

Papa's sister had brought her young sons to the safety of her family home in the country, and her husband, an art teacher at a Vienna high school, had followed suit.

'Why doesn't Uncle Erwin have to go to war?' I wondered.

'Your uncle isn't well enough for work, let alone for being a soldier,' was Mama's reply.

I never did find out what illness my uncle was suffering from. Perhaps it was something catching as he didn't mix with the patrons and even had his meals taken up to his room. It seemed fair that the doctor and the headmaster should be exempt from military service as they were desperately needed at home. Count Thurn and our '*Ortsgruppenleiter*', Herr Heidrich, were also quite indispensable; one had to look after his estate, the other after Rastenfeld council. But Uncle Erwin, from what I could see, wasn't needed urgently anywhere. He seemed well enough to cycle to neighbouring villages in order to give slide shows or take photographs of the farmers' children but wouldn't be seen dead helping at the bar or anywhere else in the house. So Grandfather and Grandmother kept struggling on with the help of Auntie Rosi and Nina, the Polish maid.

Arriving at Friedersbach one summer Sunday, Mama and I sensed that there was something seriously wrong. For a start, Barry wasn't there to greet us and Grandfather, far from his jovial self, sat at the kitchen table twisting his cap in his hands. He looked quite forlorn and seemed unaware that his pipe had gone out.

Grandmother wasn't bustling around either. She had red eyes and said hello with a croaky voice.

'They've drafted Willi!' she finally burst out.' Wouldn't even let him finish college . . . He's only a lad . . . Far too young to be a soldier!'

I slipped out of the kitchen and ran into the yard. Throwing my arms around big Barry, I buried my face in his shaggy coat and cried and cried.

Willi's being trained for the war in the desert.' Grandmother sounded very distraught on our next visit to Friedersbach. And within weeks Papa's youngest brother, my idol, was fighting in Rommel's tank division in North Africa.

'I wish they'd treated us like that in France during the last war!' Once again Opa was eyeing the army truck pull up outside our house. Under the watchful eyes of several armed guards and the admiring glances of the local girls, a dozen or so French POWs were marched into the pub's dance hall

Döllersheim church in whose cemetery Hitler's grandmother is buried.

where the monthly film show was about to begin. You couldn't really blame Opa for disliking the French as he had suffered a great deal as a soldier in France.

'Can't think why they bother,' he would carry on grumbling.' Not even their officers will know enough German to follow the film. So what's the point of bringing them, I ask you?'

'Intimidation and demoralisation, most likely,' was Omi's answer. (Why did grown-ups always have to use long, incomprehensible words?) Forget the feature film. It's the newsreels they want them to see. You don't need much knowledge of the German language to get their message: run-away victories by our soldiers and defeat and humiliation for the enemy.'

I'd heard that the French POWs in question were kept in a camp at the Truppenübungsplatz Döllersheim. This huge army training ground, only a few kilometres down the road, was strictly taboo for every civilian, Opa had said.

Opa often talked about the days when Döllersheim farmers had been his best customers. He couldn't understand why straight after the 'Anschluss', 9,000 acres of the Waldviertel's best farmland had been confiscated by the Wehrmacht, the farmers forcefully resettled and their villages razed to the ground. There was enough infertile scrubland towards the Czech border, so why pick this area to make it into the largest artillery

The ruins of Döllersheim with the artillery range now used by the Austrian army.

range of the Reich? But Döllersheim was said to be the Führer's personal choice and nobody argued with Adolf Hitler.

It was well past my bed-time when the French POWs were loaded into their truck and taken back to their camp in Döllersheim. But I couldn't help thinking about those sad looking young men in their prison uniforms who were our confirmed enemies. Surely, a nation who produced such brilliant bikes couldn't be all bad.

Some time that autumn a letter arrived from Uncle Joschi. He said he was worried about his wife and baby daughter in Vienna and wanted them to move back to Rastenfeld. Could Mama possibly find accommodation for them in the village? Mama agreed with my grandparents that there was plenty of room in our house since Frau Kurz and her children had left. So, to my great joy, Aunt Milli and 14-months-old Heidi, wide-eyed, mischievous and surprisingly fast on her little feet, came to live with us. At last I had the 'baby sister' I'd longed for all my life.

By then I'd become doubtful about the roles of Stork, Christ Child and Easter Bunny but kept up the pretence for little Heidi's sake.

NINE

THE SUMMER OF V.I.P. VISITS

One spring day in 1941 Frau Hartmann told us that something quite wonderful was going to happen in Rastenfeld:

'We have it from a reliable source that, on his way from Berchtesgaden, the Führer will honour our area with his visit,' she beamed. 'He will inspect the troops at Döllersheim and call at Rastenfeld on his way back.'

'This is a great privilege indeed and we must do everything to show the Führer our love and appreciation, in other words, the true spirit of our people. The school will play a major part in the celebrations and I expect you to give your best.'

'I've been waiting for you, Jutta,' Frau Hartmann greeted me the next morning at the school gates. 'Herr Ortgruppenleiter and I have decided that you should make the presentation to our Führer. You will stand with your mother and, when she tells you, you will walk up the steps to the podium, curtsy and offer a posy of flowers to our Führer. Do you understand?' I nodded, suddenly feeling weak in my knees. Dashing home after school I broke my big news to Mama.

'You mustn't worry, dear,' she said, stroking my hair. 'I'll be right behind you.'

The following morning the headmaster spoke to all pupils assembled in the school yard. Announcing the Führer's visit, he then explained the order of the day.

'You have to work hard and behave exemplarily from now on,' he said. 'The more merit marks you collect, the better a place you'll have on the day. But wherever you stand,' he continued, 'the great man's eyes will be upon you. And just as Jutta Schweighofer will present the Führer with flowers, each one of you will present the very best of yourself.'

Weeks of meticulous planning and rehearsing followed the headmaster's announcement and, naturally, the Führer's visit was talk number one in Rastenfeld. The excitement increased as the great day drew nearer.

Then came the let-down.

'Due to a change of schedule the Führer's visit to the Waldviertel had to be cancelled,' Frau Hartmann said, trying very hard to conceal her disappointment. 'But all is not lost as the Gauleiter will take his place. The

Gauleiter is very important and works closely with the Führer, you know.'

A long and detailed lesson on Dr. Jury followed. He was the man in charge of our home county, the Gau Nieder-Donau, which, including the capital city Vienna, formed the largest and most important part of the Ostmark. It was all extremely boring.

The day itself proved anything but. Our village looked brighter and more colourful than I'd ever seen it before. Every house was decorated with fir garlands and flowers and from every roof flew the swastika flag. A podium with the Führer's picture, flanked by two tall standards, had been erected on top of the square and the huge red banner above it read: 'Willkommen, Gauleiter!' The whole village thronged with excited people, all waiting to greet the great man and his entourage.

Women in the Waldviertel's navy-and-red dirndl dress and Hitler Youth and B.D.M., little swastika flags on the ready, lined the street. Schoolboys in white knee-socks and lederhosen and schoolgirls wearing dirndls and flowers in their hair took up their positions near the podium, ready to entertain the Gauleiter with song and dance. Choreographed and drilled by Frau Hartmann, all dances were based on folk songs and nursery rhymes. For some strange reason I still remember the 'Haversack dance' whose words went like this:

> *'Ein kleiner Schelm bist du,*
> *Weisst du, was ich tu?*
> *Ich steck dich in den Habersack*
> *Und binde oben zu.*
> *Und wenn du dann noch schreist:*
> *"Ach bitte, mach doch auf!"*
> *Dann bind' ich nur noch fester zu*
> *Und setz' mich oben drauf.'*

> (You're such a little rogue,
> D'you know what I shall do?
> I'll put you in the haversack
> And tie it up on top.
> And if you go on crying:
> 'Oh please, do open up!'
> I'll fasten the knot tighter still
> And sit on top of you.)

Slightly humiliating for the boy pushed into the – imaginary – sack and sat upon, but very enjoyable for the girl to put him in this position. For me it was sweet revenge on my partner, Klaus Piffe from Essen, for treading on my toes so many times during rehearsals. But the joyful Haversack dance could not dispel the butterflies in my stomach which had gathered there, reminding me of the task I had yet to perform.

Mama's gentle nudge signalled my moment of glory. With my knees knocking and everyone's eyes upon me, I mounted the steps to the platform. It was crowded with men in brown uniforms, all wearing swastika armbands. I curtsied – and almost presented my posy of cornflowers and marguerites to the wrong man. Herr Heidrich's hand at my elbow, I was gently propelled towards the tall, imposing figure at centre stage. Curtsying again I shyly offered my posy. What happened then completely overwhelmed me. Holding the flowers in one hand Dr. Jury patted my head with the other. Then he lifted me up, planting a kiss on my cheek. Everyone cheered and I felt my face turn very hot. Forgetting my final curtsy I hastily backed down the steps, glad to merge into the anonymous crowd of my fellow pupils.

It was pretty hard for all of us to remain motionless for what followed: Herr Heidrich's welcome for his honoured superior and the Gauleiter's long, passionate speech; but, as Frau Hartmann had stressed so many times, we were disciplined children of the great German Reich and knew our duty.

More speeches followed, more rousing patriotic songs. The whole afternoon was filled with chanting, singing and flag-waving by a spirited crowd. The euphoria

Our family at the time of Papa's stay in Vienna's Rossau garrison (summer 1942).

40

remained long after the chauffeur driven limousines had made their last lap of honour and, rounding the corner by the church, finally disappeared from sight.

The summer of 1941 brought another V.I.P. visit, even more important for our family: Papa, returning from France, was to be sent to the Rossau garrison in Vienna to receive special training for his next posting. Where this would be remained secret, but Mama had a nasty suspicion it meant Operation Barbarossa, the new campaign in the east. Whatever the future might hold for him, Papa wouldn't let it spoil the present. He was delighted over the chance to spend some time with his family in his home town. I could hardly wait for the summer holidays when Mama and I would move into Omi's Vienna flat to be near Papa. It was my first visit to the city of my birth and the initial impression was not too favourable. I hated the noise and smells of the crowded streets and the stifling heat of the concrete jungle.

For our first weekend together Papa had planned a visit to Schönbrunn, the summer residence of Austrian emperors. But at only seven-years-old I didn't appreciate the palace's splendour; its delightful surroundings were more in my line. I was truly impressed by the vast, formal gardens with dazzling flowerbeds in strict geometrical fashion, the perfectly manicured, weed-free lawns and the trees in the shape of pyramids and upturned plant pots. What I didn't like were the numerous signs: 'Betreten verboten!' How could you appreciate gardens without smelling the flowers or walking on the grass?

'Let's go to the zoo,' suggested Papa. 'I'm sure you will enjoy that.' I jumped for joy. How exciting to see all the exotic creatures I only knew from my picture books. Lions snoozing in the midday heat, seals juggling balls and hoops in more pleasant watery surroundings, chimpanzees indulging in tea-parties and hundreds more.

'See if the elephants like these!' Papa unwrapped some sugar lumps from his pocket. And I watched with delight as the rubbery trunk of a gentle giant picked them up one by one, begging for more. But the cigarette end offered by the lad next to me was ignored by Jumbo. He turned and trotted off in disgust but was back in no time with a trunk full of water. And everyone laughed and applauded when his tormentor was drenched to the skin.

The following Sunday we spent in the Prater, Vienna's vast fairground, and a paradise for the average child. Not for me, as the familiar motion-sickness kept recurring and spoilt all my fun. The only ride I could tolerate was the slow-moving Giant Ferris Wheel.

'Vienna looks much better from the air,' I announced, pressing my nose against the gondola window. Relieved to see the colour return to my cheeks, Mama smiled and agreed. She began to point out the city's various landmarks homing in on the centre.

St. Stephen's Cathedral, Vienna.

'Can you see the circle with all the green patches around it? That's the Ringstrasse with its famous buildings and parkland. And the tall church with the single spire right in the middle is the Stefansdom. Affectionately the Viennese call it "Our Steffe" or, because of its shape, "God's Index Finger".'

I was truly taken by St. Stephen's, the 'Finger of God', towering above everything else in the city. The 'Karskirche' where Mama and Papa were married, was to become my next favourite church. Unlike Our Steffe, it was very ornate, with an enormous, round dome and an interior crowded with golden angels and saints. Walking through the parks of the centre we came across the monuments of the Empress Sissi and the waltz king, Johann Strauss.

'Pity we can't see the white horses perform in the Hofburg,' Mama remarked as we approached the Imperial Palace. 'I read in the paper that the Lipizzans were taken to a safe place in Bohemia a few months ago.' The Hofburg's huge wrought-iron gate led into a square called Michaeler Platz. Entering Herrengasse from there, I was shown the large government building which housed Omi's former office. Then we called on the Trappl family in the 'Kohlmarkt' just round the corner. Sylvester Trappl was a second cousin and, while studying in Vienna, Papa had lived with him and his wife, Mitzi. I heard that, despite the long way to his college, Papa had walked there most of the time to save on tram fares. Much better than the Amalien Baths where Papa had worked as a student, I liked the bathing beach of the 'Old Danube', Omi's favourite haunt. Like the Vienna Woods it held many nostalgic memories of my parents' courting days.

'This is where I worked before we were married.' Mama pointed out a large shoe shop in Mariahilfer Strasse. 'But I see it's not called "Friedemann's" any longer.'

'Friedemanns left for America in '39, not long after "Kristallnacht",' explained Albine Bauer, Mama's friend and former colleague. 'All their shops are state property now.'

'What's "Kristallnacht", Papa?' My question seemed to take my father aback.

'Don't you worry your little head about "Kristallnacht",' he said. Then he started talking about something else. It wasn't until after the war that I found out what happened to Jewish property during 'The Night of Broken Glass'.

We spent a lovely afternoon at Aunt Albine's fancy goods shop on the Gürtel and left laden with gifts, all unobtainable in the country. And the gilt pocket mirror, the pink brush-and-comb set and the small leather purse remained my most treasured possessions for the following years.

By late August I had got used to city life and would have rather stayed put than face school with Frau Hartmann. But, as Mama assured me, it was a lot worse for Papa. For him, leaving Vienna meant leaving for Russia.

TEN

THE JEWISH-BOLSHEVIK ARCH-ENEMY

It looked like another Blitzkrieg. Again, within a few short weeks, our army had advanced into enemy territory with lightning speed. Documentary after documentary showed German panzer divisions thrusting eastwards into Russia, crushing any Soviet resistance, and excited news readers raved about the Wehrmacht's run-away victories over an inferior, ill-prepared Red Army:

'The towns of Minsk and Smolensk are in German hands . . . Our soldiers are advancing on Leningrad in the very north and, simultaneously, on Odessa in the far south of the Soviet Union . . . The Wehrmacht has captured the Ukranian capital Kiev . . . The Crimean peninsula is cut off from the rest of Russia . . .'

With their ears to the wireless, my family eagerly swallowed up the news; understandable, as Papa, too, was involved in Germany's new eastern campaign.

'Made it as far as Kiev,' read Papa's first letter from the Ukraine, 'and found most locals surprisingly German friendly. They are welcoming us as their liberators and cannot do enough for us. So, please, don't worry; I'm fine.'

Naturally, Germany's fight against Russia was also a main topic at school. It was portrayed as a black-and-white war, good against evil. Although I should have concentrated on copying from my primer I could not help overhearing what Frau Hartmann told the older pupils about 'Operation Barbarossa':

'More than 800 years ago the German emperor Friedrich Barbarossa, so called because of his red beard, marched against the Slavs. Their tribes were so inferior to his own excellent troops, that he won battle after battle and conquered vast areas of Slavic land. To gain vital living space for our German people and, at the same time, wipe out the evil of Communism for good the Führer followed Barbarossa's example in crushing the sub-human Slavs. If not defeated in his own country the Slavic-Bolshevik enemy will invade the fatherland, kill or enslave our people and destroy our culture and the German way of life.'

Posters, plastered all over the classroom walls, illustrated the teacher's words in the most drastic manner. I was really scared of those hordes of black-haired, narrow-eyed savages descending on peaceful towns and villages, looting and destroying everything in their way. In those days my evening prayers would always end in the desperate plea: 'Please, please, dear God, do let us win the war so that the "Enemy from the East" never sets foot in our fatherland.'

Another subject the propaganda cartoonist revelled in was the second arch-enemy of the Reich, the Jew. You could tell from the way they were portrayed in books and posters that Jews were inferior to the rest of us. Their prominent hooked noses, shifty dark eyes and black hair and beards gave them an unclean and most sinister appearance. To distinguish them from our people, Jews had to wear the Star of David, Frau Hartmann said. They were also forbidden to marry Germans so they couldn't pollute the pure Aryan race.

With the images of 'sub-human' Slavs and Jews in mind I began to worry about my own brown eyes, Mama's dark hair and our high cheek-bones. Omi jokingly called these features our 'Slavic legacy', as both our families originated in Czechoslovakia. At least our Aryan certificate revealed no trace of Jewish blood. Jews rarely lived in country areas, Frau Hartmann said, they found the towns better suited for their decadent practices. Rich and influential themselves, they were hell-bent on exploiting their employees and tenants and on generally suppressing the poor. The Jews didn't like it when the Führer came to power, restoring equality and justice and providing work for everyone, and thousands emigrated to other countries, taking their fortunes with them. Wasn't it right that those who stayed should contribute to the common good of the fatherland? We were told – and approved – of new camps where criminals and anti-Reich elements like Jews, communists, traitors, robbers, child molesters and other perverts would be made to work for Germany. The true nature of these concentration camps was never revealed to the average German. Yet enough was known to instil fear in people not to say or do anything contradictory to Nazi doctrine.

There was a ditty going round in our school which went:

> 'Lieber Gott, mach mich stumm,
> dass ich nicht nach Dachau komm'
>
> (Dear God, strike me dumb
> so that I shan't be sent to Dachau)

The first eye-witness report about a concentration camp reached our family through Opa's sister, who farmed near Mauthausen.

'I don't know what's going on in that camp,' I heard her say to Opa. 'They're bringing people in by the train load. Mostly Dutch Jews, I'm told; men, women and children. You can't imagine the filth of these cattle trucks. And as for the poor devils who're made to work in that quarry! Walking skeletons they are, often too weak to hold a shovel. You should see SS guards knock them about. Watching them makes my blood boil . . . '

'For God's sake, Agnes,' Opa interrupted his sister, 'keep your mouth shut about that. The wrong people might listen and you yourself will end up in a camp!'

No one had noticed me in my little corner. My nose in a book, I pretended not to have heard what was said. But the concentration camp scene, so vividly painted by my great-aunt, began to haunt me. Skeletons with shovels and pick-axes and brutal SS men with rifles and whips invaded my dreams and made me wake up screaming.

'No more reading in bed, young lady!' Mama said, and took away my book. She didn't know and I never let on what I'd heard of those terrible work camps.

Operation Barbarossa wasn't a Blitzkrieg after all, far from it. By November 1941 our panzers' stunning advances into Soviet territory had stalled as the Wehrmacht faced an additional enemy, the perilous Russian winter. 'Take Moscow or perish!' was Hitler's message as our unprepared soldiers strove to secure permanent winter quarters in the Soviet capital.

People at home were urged to support the 'Winterhilfswerk' by purchasing badges, Christmas decorations and small wooden toys. The proceeds of this new charity were to benefit our troops on the eastern front. We parted with our last warm clothes and blankets, and every woman in the village was knitting socks, gloves and balaclavas for some unknown soldier in Russia. Having mastered the art of knitting at last I, too, made my contribution in the form of dozens of multi-coloured woolly scarves.

Communications with our fighters in the east kept deteriorating. And, with postal deliveries rare and patchy, we became more and more concerned over Papa's well-being. Employed in the supply section of his division, he was bogged down in southern Ukraine where temperatures had plummeted to –40 degrees. Papa's earlier letters had told about the difficulties the Wehrmacht faced in getting food and other necessities through to their eastern armies. With the Russian rail gauge different from the rest of Europe, deliveries by train had proved problematic right from the start; they solely relied on the roads, poor at the best of times, but now virtually impassable. After the heavy truck-wastage rate caused by the foul weather, their only means of transport were horse-drawn carts and sledges. Papa always tried to keep his letters positive and light-hearted but one could read between the lines how crucial the Wehrmacht's situation had become during that hazardous Russian winter.

ELEVEN

SOME MOTHERS DO HAVE THEM

At home, too, winter had arrived early. October 1941 was a most dismal month with continuous rain and sleet, and by November Rastenfeld was snowed under. Blizzards, sweeping through the Waldviertel with uncontrollable force, had blocked the roads, brought down power lines and cut off Rastenfeld from the rest of the world. For weeks there was no electricity, no post bus and therefore no mail. But who cared about such trivialities when you had early Christmas holidays and could enjoy endless fun in the snow?

'They're drilling in the square again.' Opa, dragging in dirty boots from the orchard, tried unsuccessfully to avert Omi's attention from his sodden state. The scene was familiar: soldiers from the Döllersheim army training ground frequently spilt over onto the neighbouring villages. Mostly new recruits and mere boys, they were being drilled in all weathers to prepare them for active service in the east.

'Attention! By the right! Quick march! Left turn, one, two, three, four . . . !' As the sergeant major's bawling drowned every other noise in the village, the farmers gathered behind their net curtains to watch the spectacle in front of them. From her shop which overlooked the village green Frau Brandtner had the best view of all. She soon got to know the faces of the soldiers, above all that of Private Gotsch. One of those unfortunate recruits who, for the world, could not get his timing right, he was constantly bullied by the sergeant major.

'I'll break you, you horrible little man! I'll lick you into shape if it kills me!' His irate voice nearly cracked as poor Gotsch, by then soaked to the skin, was made to plunge into the slush yet again.

That was the moment when Frau Brandtner could take no more. Hands on hips, the little woman planted herself in front of the burly instructor.

'If this lad isn't good enough to be a soldier, just send him home!' she shrieked. 'His mother will only be too glad to have him back with her!' It was a situation the sergeant major couldn't handle. Red in the face, he ordered his men to fall out and, within minutes, marched them back to base. From that day on he was never again seen drilling in the square where the woman from the grocer's shop could be watching.

Although her heart was in the right place, Frau Brandtner could be quite tough and was well known in the village for speaking her mind. Her mother's single-mindedness and the example of her friends, mostly boys, must have rubbed off on little Ulli. Within a few short years the placid baby had grown into a determined, independent youngster, fearless of anyone or anything, who would stamp her feet and toss her curls in defiance of her less daring elders, including me. Ulli could get herself into endless trouble but somehow always escaped unharmed.

As usually, Rastenfeld's best sledge-run was the main street, fast and slippery and mostly traffic-free. You could start sledging by the Ortsgruppenleiter's house and continue down hill towards Friedersbach for two kilometres or more. Unfortunately, children my age and younger were not allowed on that 'dangerous' run. We had our own 'snowy mountain', in the very centre of Rastenfeld.

In a combined effort to secure access to their houses and, at the same time, keep the main street clear, the farmers had piled up the snow in large mounds in the square. The heaps soon knitted together, forming an extensive snowy wall. It grew so high that even the tallest person walking between the houses and the wall was totally obscured from sight. It was hard work to drag a sledge up the steps carved into the 'mountain's' sheer face but great fun tobogganing down the other side. What's more, this sledge run was considered quite safe, even for young children.

'I'm very busy with the Christmas rations just now,' Frau Brandtner had

Ulli Brandtner and myself with our mothers and Max (1942).

approached me one day. 'D'you think you could keep an eye on our Ulli?' 'Alright,' I agreed. 'She can come sledging with me.' I soon came to regret this decision. After half an hour of fun I suddenly realised Ulli was missing. My frantic search was unsuccessful; none of the other children had noticed her absence. Then a cry pierced the air. We all looked around, startled. In horror we watched the bus moving off with a small girl hanging from its ladder. As it gathered speed down the Friederbach road Ulli could hold on no longer. She let go and landed, face down, on a pile of soft snow on the roadside.

Having examined the limp little body the doctor finally turned to Ulli's distressed mother: 'Don't worry, Frau Brandtner, she's only in shock. Nothing seriously wrong with her really. She's been incredibly lucky again.'

The only injuries Ulli had sustained were bruises and abrasions to her face and hands. Frau Brandtner heaved a sigh of relief and then gave her daughter a well deserved smack on her uninjured behind. As for me, this was the day when I finally washed my hands of Ulli Brandtner.

I would rather play with older, more sensible girls like Lieselotte. Lotte and I had much in common and enjoyed the same type of games. We changed from farmers' wives, tirelessly tending their livestock, into loving mothers, caring for their numerous dolls, and again into big stars and entertainers, acting out fairy tales for younger children. Above all we were animal crazy. Coming from the city, Lotte revelled in her new country environment with all the farm animals around her. Like me she kept several pet rabbits, but wasn't allowed a dog. However, her farmer landlord didn't object to a goat. That's how Zocka, the kid, escaped her destiny of becoming the traditional Easter roast and grew into an intriguing family pet. Lotte and I would also tend wild animals, found abandoned or injured. We were heartbroken when Hansi, the baby hare we'd successfully reared with diluted milk through an eye-syringe, suddenly died after weaning. But Pipsi, the swallow, was our success story.

I had found the fledgling with a broken wing and, with the doctor's and Lotte's help, nursed him back to health. With all the insects and attention lavished upon him by his league of friends, Pipsi had grown stronger and tamer every day. Lotte and I just couldn't imagine life without our little playmate. But Mama made us think of the future.

'What will happen to Pipsi when there aren't any more insects around? No swallow can survive our severe winter. If you really love Pipsi you must encourage him to fly south with the other birds.' Mama was right and, tearfully, we decided to return our pet bird to the wild. His wing fully healed, Pipsi was taken to the balcony and urged to fly. His excursions to the neighbouring roofs became more frequent and daring and one day he was gone. We never found out if he made it to Africa but we prayed he would.

It was years after Pipsi's departure that we adopted a more conventional pet; or rather Mitzi, the stray black-and white cat, adopted us. Extremely lazy, Mitzi never bothered our baby rabbits and wild birds – and mice were quite safe from him.

TWELVE

A CHRISTMAS STORY

'Thank God, the winter is finally over,' Papa wrote in April 1942. 'It's the spring floods that make life difficult at present.'

May saw the Wehrmacht resume their drive into Soviet territory once more. While some units raced south towards the oil-fields of the Caucasus, the bulk of the panzer force was heading east for Stalingrad. Again the newsreels exuberated with our soldiers' successes in the fight against the Reich's arch-enemy:

> 'Our troops have taken the Kerch peninsula in the Crimea . . . Sevastopol is in our hands . . . The Kharkov pocket has been eliminated and 215,000 Russians taken prisoner . . . Our panzers are advancing on Kursk near Moscow . . . The Red Army has evacuated Rostov . . . The Wehrmacht takes the major Soviet naval base on the Black Sea . . . We're only 75 kilometres from the Grozny oil-fields . . . The final offensive on Stalingrad has begun . . .'

I couldn't understand all that media hype. Hadn't our superior forces triumphed everywhere in the war? Why should it be different in Russia?

But it all changed when once again 'General Winter' sided with the Red Army against the hard-pressed German troops. Rumours spread that the Sixth Army had been cut off in the Caucasus and Russian divisions were marching towards the Ukraine.

Christmas approached. According to our teacher the feast derived from an ancient Norse cult and Frau Hartmann would revel in stories about our German forefathers celebrating the winter solstice. I myself wasn't too keen on old pagan rites. Christmas to me meant carols and lights, the scent of fir branches and gingerbread men, the crib with Baby Jesus, the Christmas tree and, of course, presents.

'I'm going to post a few more cards and then collect our extra rations. Shan't be a minute!'

Omi and I, busy making straw stars for the Christmas tree, smiled at each other. We knew from experience that Mama's daily visits to the post office and Brandtner's could take hours. Women liked to congregate at Brandtner's shop to talk about the whereabouts of their soldier husbands.

Our house, more recently, with the statue of St. Florian.

We hadn't heard from Papa for weeks. Perhaps today that letter had arrived, the one we were so desperately waiting for.

From Omi's living-room window I watched Mama make her way across the village square, battling against the blizzard. The Roman sentry on the fountain in the square looked quite comical today. Was it my imagination or had his bare legs really turned blue with the cold?

'Opa, you've got to see the state St. Florian is in! Couldn't do much fire fighting today. With that snow cap over his eyes, he can't even see that he's pouring icicles instead of water.' The snoring stopped, the newspaper fell to the ground as Opa's afternoon nap had come to a sudden end.

I knew that there was no post again when I saw Mama crossing the square, her head hanging low.

'Dear God,' I started praying, 'I don't want anything for Christmas, but please, let Papa be safe.'

Back in Omi's kitchen I thought I'd heard a knock at the entrance door. Max's sudden bark turning into a drawn-out howl confirmed my suspicion.

'What's up with that daft dog now?' Opa muttered. His nap interrupted for the second time, he decided he'd better go and investigate.

'Put on a coat, Jutta! You'll catch cold!' Omi called out. Too late! I was already half-way down the stairs. At last the lock responded to Opa's fumbling fingers. The door sprang open. There stood a man in a grey military coat trying to fend off a boisterous dog. His thin face was shaded by a peaked cap but his voice, his laugh were so familiar. It couldn't be? . . . It was!

I found myself scooped up by two strong arms and whirled round a dumbfounded granddad and a delirious dog. Just moments later a little girl flew across the village square, her match-stick legs in oversized wellingtons still dancing.

'Mama!' she shouted. 'Come quickly! Hurry! You won't believe this! Papa is home!'

It was the best Christmas of my life. The lack of presents – a book and a box of crayons were the grand total – was amply compensated by Papa's presence. While decorating the tree we'd fetched from the woods together, my father suddenly pulled something from his breast pocket. The celluloid angel was slightly dented but not the worse for wear.

'Remember this?' smiled Papa and gave me a tight hug. 'He's done his job well, my little guardian angel, hasn't he?'

On Christmas Eve Papa played Silent Night on the battered accordion which had accompanied him everywhere in the war. And for Christmas dinner the family enjoyed the goose he'd brought all the way from the Ukraine.

Dying to break in my new crayons I pestered Papa to draw something for me. Papa could draw so well and together we created numerous pictures. Naturally, he had to write into my 'Stammbuch', an album of verses and sketches of people close to my heart. I was delighted with Papa's ink drawing of Rastenfeld church and school. But it wasn't until much later that I appreciated the line he'd chosen from a Paul Keller novel: '*Heimat ist Friede*,' it read. (At home there is peace).

It was wonderful to go sledging with Papa but better still to watch him put the finishing touches to the snow sculpture guarding our front door. Papa had to stand on a ladder as the snowman was as tall as the tree next to him. How realistic he looked with his potato-and-coal eyeballs, his bucket hat and broomstick cane.

On New Year's Eve Grandfather and Grandmother laid on a little party to celebrate their eldest son's home leave. If there was a sad undertone because of Uncle Karl's and Willi's absence, they tried their best not to let it show. We enjoyed Grandmother's excellent dinner and the bottle of vintage wine opened for the occasion. Papa let me have a little sip from his glass and laughed as I was pulling a face.

In the afternoon we all set off on a sleigh ride.

'You don't know how lucky you are,' said Papa, patting Fritz and Bruno's well-rounded rumps. Then he told us the funny story of Stalin and Molotov, the Ukranian horses, which were their only means for transporting supplies.

'We did notice that one of the poor, skinny creatures was getting quite big in the midriff but thought nothing of it,' he grinned. 'Only when one morning we found three horses instead of two in the stable did we realize that Stalin was a mare!'

But Papa's account of the Russian mine-dogs made us all shudder.

'Partisans trained shepherd dogs to blow up our vehicles,' he explained. 'Explosives strapped to their backs, they'd make for our tank trenches completely ignoring heavy gun fire. Those who survived would crawl under our panzers, dislodge the pin detonator and blast the tank – and themselves – to smithereens in the process.'

Those were the only two incidents Papa mentioned about Russia. He kept war talk to a minimum, at least when I was present. But he couldn't stress often enough the godsend of a home leave at such crucial a time and his unbelievable luck to escape all that trauma. It was even luckier that Papa didn't have to return to Russia at all as Yugoslavia was his next posting. For me it was back to school once again. Only the giant snowman in front of our house kept reminding me of the wonderful Christmas with Papa.

THIRTEEN

FIRE FROM THE SKIES

'Despite the most heroic efforts of the Sixth Army and Field Marshal Von Paulus, Stalingrad has fallen,' the sombre voice of the newsreader announced one critical day in early 1943. It was Stalingrad that marked the turning of the tide. Throughout the war our armies had not been defeated. From then on they were to know nothing else. But powerful propaganda kept morale high in the hinterland where the average citizen still believed in German victory.

'Stalingrad is only a temporary set-back,' Frau Hartmann announced. 'Never mind America joining the war on the side of the enemy; our superior army will win in the end!'

I was so proud of my Uncle Willi. In a fierce battle between the Allies and Rommel's Africa Korps in Tunisia he'd rescued a wounded comrade under ferocious enemy fire. Seriously wounded himself, Willi was later awarded the Iron Cross for bravery. The battle, however, was won by the Allies, marking the beginning of German retreat from North Africa.

Another blow to German morale came with the daring daylight raids on the Reich's major cities and industries. We heard of the continuous bombardment of Berlin, Hamburg, Bremen and Wilhelmshaven and of the devastation the 'Dambusters' bouncing bombs had caused in the Ruhr valley.

But the attack of British commandos on the Reich's 'heavy water' plant at a top secret location in Norway and the resulting setback to the launching of the Führer's new wonder missiles was never mentioned. Instead, German citizens were assured through schools and media: 'Keep calm! Air superiority will be ours again as soon as Germany's new miracle weapons are unleashed on Great Britain.'

Although the Ostmark was not yet greatly affected by aerial attacks, strict black-out regulations were enforced and a stringent safety drill ensured everyone knew what to do and to avoid should our area became the target of the dreaded bombs.

'Never attract the attention of enemy planes by congregating in large crowds,' we were warned as low flying RAF bombers, bound for the German heartland, began to cross the Waldviertel with menacing regularity.

'Enemy aircraft approaching from Bratislava are expected over the area around 1300 hours,' our local radio would announce most days.

Twelve noon to two o'clock was also the time for our P.E. lesson and, breaching her own safety regulations, Frau Hartmann insisted in taking us out for sport. A race to the woods was followed by games in a special clearing and, finally, another race home in the midday sun. It was then that we always encountered the dreaded enemy planes. Their droning would evoke in us extreme panic. We'd scatter in all directions, frequently throwing ourselves to the ground. Arriving home traumatised after such an experience I had to lie down for a while before I could eat or even speak. Mama became so concerned about this, she was all set for a row with Frau Hartmann. But I kept pleading with her not to confront the teacher I feared.

In July 1943 I was finally made to part with my tonsils, the alleged cause of my continuously poor health. The operation, performed in Zwettl, would be followed by a ten days' hospital stay, our doctor said. Mama was very anxious, not only over the surgery, but also the increasing danger of air raids on our towns. The event proved less of a trauma than we had feared. Sharing a small ward with a twice removed cousin helped me a lot and, in spite of the age gap, Elsa Schweighofer became a very good friend. Following surgery, neither of us could eat solids for days, but we made the best of the situation by reading, chatting and playing games. Ignoring the frequent hooting of air raid sirens, we felt quite safe in our hospital beds. The tale of the 'Flying Carpet' even convinced me that air transport could be magic and fun.

My view changed one autumn day in 1943 when Rastenfeld came under enemy fire. Waffen SS of the Death's Head division on their way east had pitched camp in the village square. Their tanks, covered in camouflage paint, caused great excitement among local boys. But Rastenfeld's adult population was less enthusiastic over the Wehrmacht's most elite troops.

'Can't stand the arrogant bastards,' Frau Brandtner complained. 'Expect customers to stand to attention when they come in the shop. Demand to be served before everyone else and always want goods we haven't seen here for years . . .'

'Have got to get the spare bedroom ready,' Mama sounded slightly put out. 'Herr Heidrich informs me two SS officers will come to stay at our house.'

Thinking of the Mauthausen SS guards, so vividly pictured by my great-aunt Agnes, I didn't treasure the thought. But my concern was unfounded; our lodgers were quite civilised. Yet there was something really sinister about that skull-and-crossbone emblem and those strange tattoos on their arms.

One lunchtime we heard – and largely ignored – aircraft approaching the village. One enemy plane left the formation, circling at an alarmingly low altitude.

'Everyone take shelter!' we were urged by Opa and the other home-guards as the siren began to scream from the church tower. Villages didn't have air-raid shelters but every house had a cellar. Ours, comprising a wash and pump-house, was spacious and vaulted, thus providing adequate safeguard against anything but a direct hit. Following the occupants of the house, a dozen or so SS men also crowded into our cellar. We'd hardly reached the bottom when a rattle, like hail stones, hit the roof. An almighty blast followed, the ground shook and we were showered with mortar. The unthinkable had finally happened: Rastenfeld was under attack from the air. We all crouched down on the floor of the cellar, faces on knees, hands over ears. Frozen in terror, we dare neither move nor speak. The sound of a fire engine almost drowned the howl of the siren and minutes seemed hours . . .

Finally, emerging into the daylight, we were caught up in a massive stampede. Swept along in a torrent of shocked, frightened people I heard someone shout: 'They've dropped a bomb on Lang's farm and there is a fire!'

The missile had come down in a field and destroyed the barn with the harvest.

'Suppose it could have been worse,' was the farmer's stoic reaction.

'If the Tommy pilot had aimed a bit better the whole bloody village could have gone up!'

A day or two passed before Lotte and I dare visit the bomb site. The scene was quite eerie: a large yawning crater surrounded by black stubble and the remains of Lang's barn still smouldering. Spluttering from the effects of the smoke, we scrambled back to the square, which again was empty and quiet. The 'Death Heads', responsible for the air raid on Rastenfeld, had long since departed.

A new wave of Allied attacks on their city from Italian soil had brought another influx of Viennese to the Waldviertel and three more ladies came to stay at our house, a former colleague of Mama's, her sister and invalid mother.

German morale received a considerable boost when at last the launch of the V-1 flying missile was announced.

'The enemy had better watch out for the next trump card the Führer has up his sleeve,' Dr. Goebbels boasted. 'V-2 will turn the tide and secure ultimate German victory.'

But by the time this lethal long-range rocket was unleashed on London it was too late to turn the savage 'sky war' in Germany's favour.

FOURTEEN

FIGHT TO THE BITTER END

The year 1944 was to bring German defeat on all fronts. Another treacherous winter had helped the Soviets recapture Leningrad, take full control of the Ukraine and launch a successful offensive on the Crimean peninsula.

'I cannot thank God enough that Papa has escaped this inferno,' Mama kept saying.

Sepp Gutmam, our maid's husband, alas, was not so lucky. One of those unfortunate soldiers trapped in the Crimea, he was reported missing, presumed dead. Poor Hanni took the news very badly and only kept going for Otto, aged three. They never did find out when and how their dad had died. Another Crimean victim was Aunt Luise's husband, leaving her widowed with four young children.

There were alarming reports of a new guerrilla war in Yugoslavia. Luckily, Papa was not involved in Tito's partisan raid on German-occupied Zagreb. Unknown to us, he had been transferred to Italy to help fight the Allies after their surprise landing at Anzio. My uncle Willi, evacuated from his North African military hospital and later transferred to France, confirmed the news reports that his commander, Field Marshal Rommel, had been appointed Commander-in-Chief of anti-invasion measures in Europe. But even the concentration of elite German forces in the area could not stop the Allied invasion of Normandy on D-Day, 6 June. By then, although we dare not speak out loud, we knew that nothing short of a miracle could save Germany. Yet the Führer never compromised. Blaming the generals for the successive German defeats, he elected to wage war to the bitter end.

The only way to stop the carnage was to kill Adolf Hitler. I clearly recall the dramatic radio broadcast of 20 July 1944. The Führer's voice, shaken but unmistakable in its rhetoric, told the nation about the failed attempt on his life.

'A very small clique of ambitious, unscrupulous and, at the same time, criminally stupid officers have laid a plot to remove me,' he proclaimed. 'But Providence has preserved me to continue my life's work for the good of the German people.'

We heard how the suitcase bomb, planted by Colonel von Stauffenberg, had wrecked Hitler's headquarters in East Prussia but left him with only cuts and bruises. At school we were told that Von Stauffenberg and the other would-be assassins of 'our beloved Führer' were soon found out and executed for their terrible crime. But nobody knew of Field Marshal Erwin Rommel's involvement in the coup or of his choice between a hero's funeral after suicide and trial by the notorious people's court. Rommel took poison. The nation was told that the great man had died of injuries received when RAF planes attacked his staff car some weeks previously.

Meanwhile, the homeland suffered more and more devastation through continuous enemy bombardment. The logic of the RAF's ongoing attacks on the Reich's industrial centres was clear enough to all Germans, but to see the ancient show-place city of Dresden totally destroyed in the eleventh hour caused outrage throughout the nation. As the talons of the Allied Armies closed tighter around Germany's capital the bombing of Berlin continued.

The question arose: 'Will there be anything left to capture of a city totally burnt out and reduced to rubble?'

Resigned to their fate, the citizens of the great Reich watched helplessly as the nightmare progressed before their eyes. Yet there were die-hards even among the local people. It was during another visit of my great-aunt Agnes that I first heard of 'The Mühlviertel Rabbit Hunt'. The notorious name 'Mauthausen' had once again aroused my curiosity and made me eavesdrop on adult conversation.

'Don't expect you've heard of the massive break-out from our camp?' Opa was quizzed by his sister. 'As for me, I shan't forget it in a hurry.'

'Happened some weeks back when we had all that snow,' she continued.' 'The SS shot a hundred inmates straight off, then made the locals track down them still on the run. Mind you, most didn't need a lot of pressing. Quite enjoyed mowing down the poor devils, as if they were rabbits. Found a young Russian in t' barn the same night. Skinny and bare-footed he was, and frightened to death. Couldn't turn in the poor wretch, could I? Fed him and let him stay in the hay-loft till t' commotion was over. Then sent him off with a coat and warm boots of our Michael's and a rucksack of grub. Trust he's made it over the border . . .'

'You've done what, Agnes?' Opa exploded. 'Are you completely out of your mind? Compassion is one thing, but this is madness. If the SS get wind that you've helped the enemy everyone in your house will end up dead!'

I'd held my breath listening to Aunt Agnes's story. Surely, she didn't deserve that scolding from Opa. When looking up, I detected a warm glint in my granddad's eyes. I saw how proud he really was of his brave, kind sister.

That night I dreamt of watching Papa and Uncle Joschi taking part in a hunt. But their prey wasn't deer, foxes or rabbits but skeletal, barefooted men. One by one they collapsed in the hail of merciless fire. And, slowly, the white snow turned crimson as they lay twitching and dying . . .

Spring 1945 brought the Reich's final days and the bloody end to the war in Europe. Reports reached us that our soldiers, still under arms in North Italy, had been forced to surrender. Once again we were in the dark over Papa's fate. Was he still alive? Had he been taken prisoner by the Allies?

On 30 April 1945 a radio broadcast by Admiral Doenitz shook the nation: 'Our beloved Führer is dead. He fell in the brave fight against the fatherland's Jewish-Bolshevic arch-enemy . . . He fought for Germany to the bitter end despite betrayals, cowardice and lies around him . . .'

The truth was that Hitler, realising that all was lost, had killed himself in his Berlin bunker while the Russians were virtually hammering on the chancellory doors above. The charismatic leader who had seduced a whole civilised nation and was responsible for the death of countless millions had met his own destiny. Admiral Doenitz, his successor, pledged to continue Adolf Hitler's 'just' war but found little support. The slaughter was over. For my country the last few days of war brought a final senseless act of destruction: Trying to stop the Red Army crossing from Hungary, SS-troops stationed in Vienna, had blown up all the bridges over the Danube.

During the fight over the city a shell hit St. Stephen's Cathedral, destroying its roof and most of the choir vaulting. The 'Pummerin', a 20-ton bell, cast from 200 Turkish cannons, fell from the tower and shattered. And with its famous Gothic landmark, most of Vienna's very heart went up in flames. The Opera House was on fire, so was the Burgtheater and Parliament House. The palaces of Schwarzenberg, Schönbrunn and Belvedere scored direct hits and such was the damage that restoration was not completed until ten years later. Above all, the short battle over Vienna claimed heavy human casualties, and 130,000 of our soldiers were taken prisoner.

On 13 April 1945, seven years and one month after the Anschluss, Austria's capital was liberated by the Red Army. Instead of the Swastika the Hammer and Sickle now flew from all government buildings. It was now that the real suffering began in the city as the Viennese found themselves at the mercy of a victor whose revenge for German atrocities against his own people knew no bounds.

The Waldviertel, too, saw incredible turmoil at the end of the war. With the north-western railway line from Vienna sabotaged by the Soviets, the roads had to take the bulk of retreating soldiers and refugees, all heading west in an attempt to escape the advancing Red Army. There were Germans from Silesia, fleeing a second time, Slovaks and Hungarians, as well as many people from Vienna and the nearby oil refineries of Zistersdorf. Count Thurn and his family had left their Rastenberg castle for the American sector in Upper Austria – or Ober-Donau as it was still called – and our Ortsgruppenleiter had also fled with his wife and daughters. They'd hardly turned their backs when their homes were broken into and looted by opportunists with a grudge against high profile Nazis and the 'idle rich'.

'That's it,' said Opa, watching a guest worker carrying a dozen pairs of the countess's shoes on his bike. 'We're definitely not leaving our home. As refugees we'd be most vulnerable and bound to lose everything. Just watch what's happening at Heidrich's house and Rastenberg castle.'

So, reluctantly, we hid our most precious possessions behind the wall Opa had built in the loft and stayed put despite fearing the worst.

My aunt Luise's views were different from Opa's. At the Russians' march on Vienna she'd packed her four children and a few belongings into a horse-drawn cart and headed west for the safety of the American zone. But by the time she'd reached Upper Austria the border was closed and she and thousand others were turned back. I hardly recognized her when, after weeks on the road, she finally arrived in Rastenfeld. A deep red scar, received in an accident when her horse had bolted, disfigured her once beautiful face. She was emaciated, drained and grief-stricken. Her eldest son, Dieter, one of my earliest admirers, had died of kidney failure by the roadside. He was just 12-years-old. Moved by the poor woman's plight, Hanni Gutmann, a war widow herself, invited Aunt Luise and her family to stay at her house until conditions improved.

As all schools in the area were needed to accommodate the ever-increasing stream of refugees, some 50 nuns had vacated their town convent and moved to the already crowded Stift Zwettl monastery. The attached primary school, regarded as a safe haven between fronts, had been chosen by Gauleiter Jury as a temporary home for his family. It was there that he committed suicide in May 1945.

To accommodate the masses of refugees swamping the Waldviertel, makeshift camps were established near Zwettl. However, another serious problem arose: the water supply from springs and streams proved insufficient and was supplemented by polluted water from the Kamp. That and the appalling hygiene in the camps led to the outbreak of typhoid and dysentery in a large area around Zwettl. The authorities had no choice but to place the town under quarantine. Hundreds of country people perished as there were no ambulances or other transport to take them to hospital. By the autumn of 1945, 120 typhoid cases had been recorded in Zwettl alone and 39 locals had died from the disease. The great personal tragedy of the town's first post-war mayor was described by Josephine, our neighbour's daughter, an employee at his pharmacy: 'My boss had already lost two sons in the war and then his only daughter died from typhoid. Herr Schuller thought the world of his family, but all he's got left now is ten-year-old Hansi.'

FIFTEEN

LIBERATED BUT NOT FREE

7 May 1945 had finally brought peace to a battered Europe. As the 'Reich of a Thousand Years' lay in ruins, its people had to come to terms with not only the consequences of a lost war but also the shame of Nazi atrocities in the concentration camps discovered by the Allies.

For Austria the end of the war meant also the end of German domination but not the freedom promised at the Moscow Declaration in November 1943. Instead, the new democratic republic found itself divided into four zones occupied by the armed forces of Great Britain, the United States, the Soviet Union and France. This foreign occupation was to last for a whole decade. The re-definition of Germany's borders resulted in a major confrontation between the super-powers which became known as the 'Cold War'. As the line dividing the two mighty blocs ran right through the new Austria, my country's fate was inevitably weighed against the tensions between East and West. My home-province, Lower Austria, alas, was destined for Soviet occupation and so was, until later, the whole of Vienna.

The desperate situation in our capital city only became clear to us when one day, completely out of the blue, Aunt Milli's younger sister, Herma, appeared on our doorstep. Sobbing and shaking with exhaustion and relief she poured out a story of personal tragedy:

Her father had been killed in the air-raid which destroyed their villa at the eleventh hour. Her mother, rescued from the rubble, sustained a total breakdown and was later transferred to a mental institution. At work when the bomb wrecked her home, Herma herself had escaped with her life but become more and more desperate to flee the city where starvation and disease were rife and women suffered so much at the hands of the merciless invaders.

Her hope that she would be able to join her sister in the country was dashed after trains stopped ruining and all other means of transport, including bicycles, were requisitioned by the 'liberators'. The crunch came the day she and some other girls had been forced at gun point to accompany a group of Russian soldiers to a dance hall. Narrowly escaping her drunken captors, Herma had just started walking. Like most women fugitives she'd hid in the woods during daylight and moved only at night until, after weeks on the road, she finally reached Rastenfeld. How could we refuse her shelter?

AUSTRIA: ZONES OF OCCUPATION

1945-55

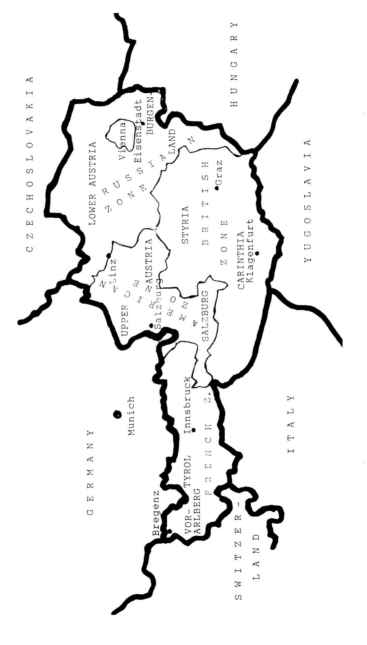

But our house was slowly running out of space so I had to share my bedroom with Aunt Herma. Fascinated by the elegant, artistic redhead, I soon became her most adoring fan. We had regular bed-time story sessions, followed by serious 'adult' conversation. But I could never get my roommate to talk about her latest experiences in Vienna.

Not long after Herma's arrival the Red Army reached the Waldviertel. The last locally stationed troops, unsuccessful in fleeing to the Americans in Upper Austria, surrendered immediately. Taken prisoner, they were confined to a huge camp near Stift Zwettl and later deported. However, one or two daring soldiers managed to escape capture.

'There is something odd about Kerschbaum's new farmhand,' Frau Brandtner confided in Mama. 'Has a peculiar name and a Prussian accent . . . Said to be an SS man; had his tattoo taken out by the doctor . . .'

The rumours surrounding Olaf Malschucke were never proven. He later married his employer's daughter and became postmaster in Rastenfeld.

The first Soviet action on reaching the Waldviertel was to confiscate all the 'properties of the Reich'. The largest one, the Döllersheim's army training ground, became the main accommodation for Russian troops. Their officers, however, enjoyed the luxury of private villas. A whole residential suburb of Zwettl was requisitioned for the higher ranks and their families who soon came to join them. Unbelievable stories began to spread about the occupying forces in the next town.

'Have you heard, they're keeping pigs in the living-room of No 5, Parkstrasse?' enquired a neighbour.

'Our liberators don't seem to know what bathrooms are for,' sniggered another. 'They use basins and bath tubs as toilets and wash vegetables in the W.C.!'

Few people believed the gossip until the owners, eventually allowed to return to their homes, confirmed those incredible tales.

There were drunken orgies in the convent, also occupied by the Russians. On one occasion intoxicated vandals raided the biology lab, smashed the ampulas containing animal preparations and drunk the preserving fluid. And eye-witnesses described the river Zwettl in the town centre as a stinking mass of dead trout, caused by the Soviet method of fishing by hand-grenade.

It was not long before the food shortage we'd managed to escape throughout the war hit the Waldviertel. Their crops destroyed, their fields confiscated and turned into refugee and POW camps, the local farmers could hardly feed themselves, let alone the thousands of inmates and members of the occupying forces in the area. Many had been robbed of their carts and horses on their way to work, their women molested and their farms looted in their absence. Understandably, even those still in possession of their own transport dare not turn out to tend their fields. Food sent to Lower Austria by the more affluent western counties was often intercepted by modern highwaymen, thus failing to reach the area it was destined for.

On 9 May, one day after the official end of the war, the first Russian soldiers entered Rastenfeld.

'What a stupid sign Dr. Gruber has had put up at the village entrance,' a neighbour observed. (Dr. Gruber, a retired vet who'd lived in Rastenfeld since before the war, had taken over as temporary Bürgermeister.)

The huge placard draped across the road welcomed our liberators in German and Russian. Nobody could understand the strange scrawl, produced by Herr Cerveny, the policeman, who had some knowledge of the Russian language The German translation, however, was clear enough. It read:

'DOWN WITH THE GERMANS! LONG LIVE THE RED ARMY!'

I was totally confused by this message. All my young life I'd been made to believe that Germans were 'tops' and the Russian barbarians our worst enemy. Now suddenly this reversal of thinking. Other villagers must have felt the same as the account of the first act of 'Soviet liberation' brought a faint smile to many a worried face: Dr. Gruber, at the head of the welcoming party, had been instantly relieved of his wrist watch.

There was very little to smile about in Rastenfeld over the months to come as our 'liberators' turned out to be almost as bad as portrayed by the Nazis. From his chosen residence, the Ortsgruppenleiter's house, the Russian commandant soon established a reign of terror. He and his all-male staff frequently threw wild drinking parties, enlisting the company of women. But as there were never enough volunteers, local girls would be 'invited', sometimes at gun point, to take part in these noisy, all-night drunken rave-ups. Too young to appreciate the threat to our women I was more concerned over Mama's increasingly strange behaviour.

If any man asks you how old you are, you say you're seven,' she'd urge me. But why should I pretend to be much younger if Mama herself looked like 100?

These days she'd never leave the house without dusting her hair with flour and putting on a head-scarf and a long, dowdy skirt. In fact, the entire village population seemed to consist of old women in tatty clothes walking with a stoop. We all were most reluctant to venture out into the square as the commandant, when drunk, would shoot aimlessly from his first floor windows, making everyone scatter and dive for shelter.

One day the historic pillory in the village centre fell victim to a Russian machine-gun attack. Its massive stone ball, once chained round the neck of an unfortunate victim, lay now shattered on the ground. Rid of this relic of medieval torture, our people were made to suffer more updated cruelty in 1945.

For the commandant the gun was also a means of communication.

'There goes the Russian taxi service again,' Opa would say as three shots in close succession rang out, and the doctor, the only villager with a car, rushed from his surgery to resume his role of the commandant's chauffeur. His wife and patients lived in constant fear that some day he might not return from one of those secret looting trips. With the legal representative of the occupying force setting such bad example, stray hordes of Russian soldiers were allowed to haunt the area unchecked, pillaging, looting and generally terrorising our people. Yet now and then, in desperation the worm would turn. It was on one of our now rare visits to Friedersbach that I heard of such a macabre case.

'Something awful happened to the Mitterers', Minna.' Grandmother's voice was reduced to a whisper. 'Promise you won't breathe a word of this. Two Russians turned up at their farm the other week. Demanded 'vino', then started pestering the girls. Marianne locked herself in the cellar, so the pair of them set on my goddaughter, Laura. Dragged her into the barn and almost strangled her as she struggled and screamed. The poor lass must have passed out for a while. Came to with a start when a heavy weight came down on her. It was a dead weight, a body with a pitch-fork stuck in his back! A terrible fight was going on next to her. Then, all of a sudden, the other Russian caved in. Hadn't reckoned with brother Markus who'd been mucking out in the stable next door. Big, strong lad, Markus, and short-tempered, too. Wasn't having his sister molested . . . Waited till dark, then buried the villains. Kept quiet about it and up to now no one's found out . . .'

Grandmother's grisly tale left me shocked and bewildered. What on earth was it the Russians were after? Why did they always harass women and girls?

If that's what peace was all about, I would have rather had war. Even through a trusting child's eyes, our future looked barren and bleak.

Rastenfeld Square with the church and (in front) the house where the Russian commandant took office in 1945.

SIXTEEN

THE DARKEST NIGHT

'Would you mind if Lieselotte stayed with you overnight? I Aunt Herta asked Mama one day in late May. 'As you know, we've got Russians camping in our orchard and there might be trouble. They couldn't possibly get into your house. Your door is so much safer than ours.'

I hopped with excitement when Mama said yes and helped her put up the camp-bed in my room. I liked it when Lotte, my very best friend, came to stay. We had giggled and talked and hardly dropped off to sleep when suddenly we were startled by a strange noise and Max's barking. Bleary-eyed, I saw Mama stand by my bedside, her forefinger against her lips.

'There is somebody at the front door,' she whispered. 'We'd better tell Omi and Opa. Quickly, get up but don't make a noise!'

Clad only in our night-dresses, Lotte and I stumbled upstairs after Mama. My grandparents ushered us into their kitchen where most of the other occupants of the house had already gathered. We all huddled together, wondering what to do next.

'It's no good, I'll have to open the door,' said Opa as the hammering grew more vehement by the minute. 'I'll hold them up as long as I can while you make your get-away through the back.'

We all crept downstairs, heading for the passage which led to the fields. But our escape route was blocked. Opa had forgotten that, because of the Russians in the neighbouring orchard, he'd secured the back gate with an additional padlock.

There was panic, increased by a terrific crash. The heavy oak door, reinforced with sheet metal, had finally given way, and a dozen or more soldiers were pouring into the yard.

Women scattered in all directions, desperate for a place to hide. Mama, Lieselotte and I just managed to dive behind the mortar-pan, a large wooden container, propped against the shed wall next to the limepit. Max went berserk. Snarling, he jumped at one of the raiders. A shot rang out followed by a howl, then eerie silence. With a quick hand over my mouth Mama stifled my scream. Through the gaps between my fingers I saw several soldiers dash upstairs pushing aside a protesting Opa. Others made straight for the rooms on the ground floor. Doors slammed and windows crashed as they hauled one after another of our belongings to the army truck in front of the house.

Meanwhile, a search party of three or four Russians had begun to comb the yard and the outbuildings. Screams pierced the darkness as women, tracked down one by one, were chased by the invaders. Aunt Milli most certainly owed her escape to her daughter. No hardened soldier, it seemed, could bear the heart-rendering cries of a small child. After some arguing, little Heidi and her distraught mother were grudgingly released. Her aunt was not so lucky . . .

'Get off! Let go! You're hurting me!' The voice, the red hair shining in the torch light was unmistakable. I froze as Herma, fighting and kicking out at her captor, was dragged across the yard. But the soldier just laughed. Vice-like his grip tightened around the girl's slight body. A brutal hand clamped over her mouth and stifled her screams. Then silence as a door slammed behind assailant and victim . . . In horror, Lotte and I closed our eyes, gripping Mama's hands tighter.

The sound of rustling paper very near by made us jump. A match was struck and the face of a Russian appeared only yards from our hide-out. This was the end. If not discovered, the three of us would be burnt alive . . . Thank God, the flame proved not strong enough for detection and the soldier moved on. We had been saved by the darkness.

Minutes later Opa's contorted face, a pistol pointed to his temple, appeared in the light of the upstairs kitchen window.

'Three other women where?' bellowed a voice in broken German. The gang must have checked the beds in the house and Mama, Lotte and I were not accounted for. My teeth began to chatter and, trembling with cold and fear, I moved still closer to my mother.

'Dear God, please, please, don't let them find us . . . and, please, don't let Opa get shot! 'My prayers were answered. At dawn the intruders finally left. But it was another half hour before our benumbed trio dare emerge from our hiding place. Mama looked like a ghost. Her eyes staring, her steps slow and mechanical, she seemed oblivious to the world around her.

A loud sob escaped my lips as we passed the body of brave, faithful Max. But Mama pulled us along.

'It's all right, dears, keep going! We're safe now. Everything will be all right,' she kept saying, her arms wrapped round our trembling shoulders. Without wasting one glance on her violated home she gently led two little girls through the shattered front door.

At the Österreichers' house we met up with Aunt Milli, her sister and small daughter. Heidi was curled up on the sofa, sleeping off the ordeal of the night. But everyone's concern was with Herma. Her blouse ripped, her face bruised and streaming with tears, she couldn't stop shaking and sobbing. Anni kept making hot drinks and had run the bath water for

Herma. But even after an hour's soak she kept on whimpering: 'I feel dirty, so dirty . . .'

At last a merciful sleep had overwhelmed Herma; and Aunt Milli, Mama and I braced ourselves to face the scene of destruction at home.

We found curtains torn from the windows, lamps ripped from the ceilings and everything removable gone: carpets, eiderdowns, pillows and even the mattresses from our beds. One single handkerchief caught in the door was the pathetic remainder of two wardrobes full of linen and clothes.

Mama sat down for a while, her hands over her eyes. Then, slowly, she began to pick up the smashed plates and cups from the floor.

'They wouldn't have done that to us if Papa were home!' I burst out, seething with anger. But Papa was a long way away, a POW in Italy. He would be suffering himself, unaware of the tragic events in his homeland.

After that terrible May night of 1945 Mama and I spent many more sleeping on bare bedsteads or, worse still, hiding in woods and cornfields. And, although conditions did improve slowly, we had to endure two more attacks on our home. Thank God for Opa's partition in the attic! The raiders never discovered the false wall or anything hidden behind it.

The only good thing that happened to us children in 1945 were summer holidays of about half a year. Used as refugee shelters at the end of the war, all schools remained closed for the months to follow. By the time they opened again I had reached the age of secondary education.

But Zwettl, still in the grip of camp misery, vandalism and disease, was clearly out of my grasp. So Mama let me stay on at the village school hoping the situation would get better soon. The first thing I noticed entering the headmaster's class for the new term was a complete change in the school's decor. All pictures of the Führer and swastika flags had vanished. Instead, a crucifix hung now in every classroom.

No more mentioning of Adolf Hitler and his 'glorious deeds', no more Nazi salutes. Yet old habits die hard; despite strict instruction to use 'Grüss Gott!' only from now on, the odd 'Heil Hitler' still managed to escape the lips of some flustered pupil. Before she could be forcibly removed from her post as a staunch Nazi, Frau Hartmann had taken early retirement. Two lady teachers straight from college were now in charge of the infants and juniors. Rastenfeld school once again had three classes.

The traumatic events of 1945 had made me outgrow my childhood and mature beyond my 11 years. People also remarked on the change in my looks. My hair, now darker and worn in two long plaits, was the envy of most of my school-friends. My health had improved and, despite the food shortage, I had at last put on a little weight. But the most drastic metamorphosis was yet to come.

For a while I had noticed, but chosen to ignore, a certain difficulty in reading the blackboard. Finally, my deteriorating sight was detected and duly corrected with glasses. But, although they dramatically bettered my vision, I truly hated the wretched things.

In those days only old people like Omi and Frau Hartmann had spectacles and I felt ugly and square wearing mine.

Matters got worse when some boys in my class kept on chanting: *'Mein letzter Wille – eine Frau mit Brille!* (My last wish is a wife with glasses).

Convinced of never, ever getting married (Why should I? I could manage very nicely without men), I was still hurt by the sneer. My glasses, I decided, were for emergencies only and, for years, I got away with it.

SEVENTEEN

NUNS AND THEIR HABITS

The move to boarding school had not been easy.

'You don't expect me to take you and all that clobber,' the driver of the post bus had scoffed, leaving Mama and me with an assortment of luggage and bedding behind at the bus stop. Luckily, it was 'Fastenmeyer's day' and, as a private operator, Herr Fastenmeyer was more accommodating.

'Just get in, Missis, I'll see to your gear,' he'd grinned and shoved Mama and me into his window-less van. Negotiating the luggage piled up in the middle we sat down on wooden benches and, with the van's jerky movements, the events leading up to this trip flashed through my mind:

The first encounter with nuns at the entrance exam and my triumph to have passed for class two . . . The extra tuition from Frau Hartmann to 'top up' my maths (no getting away from the dreaded teacher!) and, by contrast, my first enjoyable English lessons from Fräulein Amalia, our parish priest's sister . . . The alarm over Mama's own embarrassment when she began: 'You are growing up, Jutta, and there are certain things you ought to know . . . '

I'd thrown myself onto my bed and cried and cried. Thinking of the dangers women were subjected nowadays I didn't want to grow up, couldn't face the uncertain adult world. But here I was, aged 11, leaving home for a remote boarding school full of strange nuns with black habits and peculiar sounding names.

Within minutes the rough ride and worry began to play havoc with my stomach nerves. Eyes tightly shut, my inside churning, I sat clutching my hankie, wishing to die. Feeling sorry for the girl who was so terribly sick, Herr Fastenmeyer dropped us off right in front of the convent and, gradually, I returned to the world of the living.

A plump, friendly nun and two girls led us into the building.

'I'm Sister Anastasia', she smiled 'and you must be – now, let me see Jutta Schweighofer from Rastenfeld, am I right? Sit down, dear, and let the colour return to your cheeks while Fritzi and Steffi see to your luggage.'

'Don't worry, Frau Schweighofer, we'll take good care of your daughter.' An encouraging wink towards Mama and the reception room door closed behind her.

There wasn't much time for tearful goodbyes as Mama had to leave within minutes to catch the last post bus home. I was whisked away by Steffi and Fritzi and shown everything I needed to know: my bed and locker in the dormitory, the washroom, day-room and dining hall. The girls helped me unpack, then demonstrated the art of bed making.

'Your eiderdown must have razor-sharp edges all around, d'you see?'

'Like a row of white coffins,' it struck me as my eyes wandered from one identical squared bed to the next. But I kept my morbid thoughts to myself. They returned with vengeance at night:

'I wish I were home in my own bed! Don't like sharing a bedroom with 20 strange girls and a nun.' Clutching Omi's farewell present, the tiny pocket-manicure set, I could no longer hold back my tears.

It was nearly midnight when the door opened and, following the beam of her torch, Sister Felicitas tiptoed towards the cubicle in the corner, her rosary jingling. Watching her oversized shadow against the white cubicle curtains, I couldn't help wondering about the peculiar garments of nuns and what hair, if any, was hidden under that tight-fitting veil.

I felt I hadn't slept at all when Sister Consolata's *'Gelobt sei Jesus Christus!'* (Praise be to Jesus Christ) shook me out of a late dream.

'In Ewigkeit, amen!' replied one or two drowsy voices. Then it was: 'Good morning, girls! It's a lovely bright day! Quickly, get up and don't hang about!'

I crawled out of bed and joined the queue for the washroom. The chill of the concrete floor and the icy cold water soon had everyone fully awake. Hot water and a heated bathroom were luxuries we were granted only once every week. Friday was bath-night and fun-night. The dormitory lights stayed on until, sparkling clean, the last girl returned and there was plenty of time for chatting and story-telling. But Sister soon stopped more energetic pursuits like 'trampolining' and pillow-fights. The only negative aspect of Friday was the kind of meal preceding bath-night with boring regularity: hot elderberry compote served with a giant boiled potato. Wild berries, cheap and easily available, played a primary part in the post-war convent diet. It was hard luck for those who couldn't stomach the medicinal elderberry taste. The nuns had no time for 'fussy eaters'. Filled to the brim, plates were passed from girl to girl and nobody left the table before they were empty. With fresh meat a rare commodity, wasting such a godsend came close to a mortal sin.

So, inevitably, fat and gristle would end up in the wash-up water for the cutlery which, half-way up the table, began to look like a revolting brown stew. UNICEF contributions of corned beef, dried milk and maize flour did help to enhance our menu, and Sister Monika, our resourceful cook, heaped maize bread, maize dumplings and Polenta upon us until it came out of our ears. I still cringe at the thought of our post-war boarding school diet and those rigid dining-room rules. The other 99 guidelines placed

Our class in the final year of secondary school at the Zwettl convent (1949). I am the fourth from the left in the middle row.

upon us by a strict convent regime did not worry me much. After all, I'd been trained by Frau Hartmann.

School was fun at the convent.

'Well done, my dear,' Sister Tarcisia would smile and reward my latest essay with yet another gold star. And Sister Camilla's praise over 'excellent work' and 'remarkable progress' in English made my ears glow with pride! Even maths became an enjoyable subject and so did P.E., consisting mainly of movement and dance. But my new flair for needlework was entirely due to the teacher. We saw a lot of Sister Imelda in her additional capacity of day-room supervisor. A gentle lady, she could be quite firm, insisting on total silence for our afternoon studies and practical application of the compulsory etiquette lessons.

But most of the time the day-room enjoyed a relaxed atmosphere where we felt at ease and 'at home'. Sister Imelda would read to us and involve us in needlework, painting and music. There was a drama group, a choir and even a five-piece band where I could show off my new skill on the guitar.

Engaging the help of Sister Tarcisia (for script and poetry), Sister Caecilia (for music and choreography) and Sister Veronika (for costumes), Sister Imelda would put on Christmas and Mother's Day concerts and Carnival fancy-dress parties. And, when it came to rehearsals, even the strict study-period rules would be waived.

In contrast with calm, patient Sister Imelda, Sister Caecilia, a former teacher of Mama's, had the temperament of the typical artiste. Through no fault of my own I once crossed her to the extent of almost stopping the show. We were rehearsing a spectacular pageant for the Golden Jubilee of the Prelate, produced by Sister Caecilia.

Fifty dancers achieved the symbolic effects of a cross, anchor and heart and a huge number 50 by synchronising colourful rods. To complete the final spectacle, sun-rays over a rainbow, some of us had to climb a number of steps to the camouflaged scaffolding at the rear. Suddenly, catastrophe struck. Only days before the event I went down with a tummy bug.

'I'm sorry, but Jutta is not well enough to carry on with rehearsals,' Sister Imelda said firmly and pulled me out of the show. Sister Caecilia nearly went through the roof! Reports about my understudy's blunders seeped through to my isolated sick-bed: 'Elfi Winter makes Sister Caecilia's blood boil. She keeps dropping her rods and has fallen off the scaffolding twice.'

But in the end they did manage without me and the show was a triumph. Yet Sister Caecilia could not forget my 'desertion'. She never cast me in the following Mother's Day play. The solo part of the Forget-me-not went to my best friend, Inge.

This tiny, vivacious girl and I had hit it off from the very first day.

'Hi, I'm Inge, Inge Lugmayr. I wish I could grow plaits like yours,' a bright voice from the bed next to mine had penetrated my gloom. Looking up I saw a pretty face with enormous brown eyes and a thatch of ultra-short hair. Inge and I soon realised how much we had in common. Gifted for arts and languages, we loved reading, drawing and music but, despite our business backgrounds, we totally lacked interest in commerce. And, although both very short-sighted, we shared an aversion for glasses. We became inseparable, sat next to each other in class, at dinner, in church and always made up a pair on the compulsory Sunday afternoon walks. The 'convent crocodile' of 100-odd girls and two nuns, winding through the narrow, cobble-stoned streets, was a familiar sight in and around Zwettl. When the silence, imposed on us in the town centre, was finally lifted, Inge and I never stopped chatting. I got to know all about the Lugmayr family from Arbesbach in the Upper Waldviertel: the lovely, artistic mother and shrewd, dominant father who had insisted on a commercial education for three of his four children. Unfair, as it seemed at the time, this proved a wise move, enabling Herbert and Günter to take charge of the family shops when their father died quite young of appendicitis. Inge had no head for business. When a Gymnasium (grammar school) was opened in barracks near our school she transferred there. But remaining a convent boarder, she continued to be my best friend.

Advent was the pinnacle of the convent year.

'Giving is better than receiving,' Sister Imelda would say, ensuring we prepared for Christmas in the right spirit.

My friend Inge, aged 14.

*Myself as a 14-year-old
(summer 1949).*

Two or three times a week we would brave the dark, frosty mornings for Rorate (first mass of the day) at the parish church in the town centre. Instead of pictures, the Advent calendar in the day-room contained useful suggestions like: 'My locker needs tidying' or 'Today I shall eat my dinner without waste and complaints'. We all loved the Engerl-Bengerl game practised throughout Advent. This meant at least one good deed a day for one's 'Bengerl' (little rascal), a girl whose name had been drawn from a hat. Unaware of her 'Engerl's' (little angel's) identity, she looked after a 'Bengerl' herself. At weekends we would congregate by the advent wreath, hear Christmas stories and sing carols. How fascinating, that the most famous of all had originated in a tiny Austrian village.

'One Christmas more than 100 years ago there was panic in Oberndorf church,' Sister Imelda told us. 'The old harmonium had given up the ghost as mice had gnawed through the bellows. The priest, Josef Mohr, was very upset; midnight mass without music was unthinkable. In the end Franz Gruber, the teacher, saved the day. Playing the guitar, he sang the carol he'd composed to Pfarrer Mohr's lyrics. A few years later 'Silent Night', translated into every possible language, had conquered the world.'

On 6 December the convent would receive St. Nicholas' visit. His robe, and long white beard could not conceal the remarkable likeness to our chaplain. But who cared about the identity of a saint who gave out rare goodies like oranges, apples and biscuits? In contrast, my birthday, following St. Nicholas Day closely, passed always unnoticed. The nuns would rather celebrate our Namenstag (saint's day). Mine, on 22 December, tended to coincide with breaking up for Christmas, so I missed out yet again.

It didn't matter. After 14 weeks at the convent I couldn't wait to join my family for Christmas at home. I was hopping with impatience for the horse-drawn sleigh to pull up at the convent. At last there was Grandfather, eyes twinkling and moustache bristling under a big furry hat.

'Guess what, Jutta,' he burst out, pulling me and my suitcase onto the sleigh. 'Your Uncle Karl's come home at long last; arrived just in time for Christmas. Mind you, he's skin and bone and quite poorly, but you know Grandmother; she'll soon have him right.'

'That's fabulous! I'm so thrilled!' I said, hugging Grandfather. Then climbing into my fur-lined sleeping bag: 'Any other family news?'

'Yes, Jutta. Rosi, Erwin and the lads have gone back to Vienna. And yesterday there was a letter from Willi. He's got a job in a place not far from Salzburg. Piesendorf, I think, it's called.'

I was so pleased for my young uncle. Still in hospital at the end of the war, he'd been released into the American zone and completed his education in Salzburg. And with the teacher shortage at present he had soon found employment.

'But Willi is coming back home again, isn't he, Grandfather?,

'Shouldn't think so, lassie, not just yet, anyway. Can't say I blame him. As things stand he's much better off where he is with the Americans.'

'And what about Papa? Any news from him yet?' For a while this question had burnt on my tongue.

'No, dear. As far as we know he's still a POW in that place in Italy with the lopsided tower.'

As soon as we'd reached the outskirts of Zwettl the road disappeared, merging with the fields of the 'Rudmanns Plateau'. It was an hour before it reappeared, sheltered by rocks and forests of the Purzelkamp valley. And there was the familiar route Mama and I had taken so often when walking in the woods was still safe. I thought of my essay: 'A Walk to Friedersbach' which had gained top marks at the entrance exam, then looked at big Barry. Curled up at our feet like a giant hot-water bottle, he had suddenly stirred. Did he remember the day when a female of the species had lured him all the way to Rastenfeld? Smiling, I pictured the end of Barry's amorous journey and his undignified return home in Grandfather's cattle-wagon.

I almost missed the Herrgott-Stein under its bulging white cover but, reaching the dip where our favourite sledge-run had always ended, I knew that Rastenfeld was only minutes away. Oh, the joy of being home again. I returned Mama's tight, welcoming hug, then dashed straight upstairs into the arms of Omi.

'My God, you have grown!' she cried, looking me up and down fondly. And it filled me with pride that at the age of twelve I was now towering above my dear petite grandma.

With most of our lady lodgers gone, the house seemed more like our own again. But I did miss Aunt Milli and especially little Heidi.

'They've moved to Styria, dear,' Mama explained. 'Uncle Joschi got a job in Gusswerk near Mariazell when he came back from the war.'

I also missed Lieselotte. After three years in Rastenfeld she had gone back to Vienna with her mother and brother.

My aunt Herma was still with us but she didn't look at all well.

'Poor dear is very bad with her nerves after all she's been through,' Mama explained. 'She's not fit for work, Herr Doktor insists. Might as well stay until her health gets better.'

Our friends in the village were so pleased to see me and most had good news: Rudi Österreicher, back from France, was about to marry his sweetheart, Elli, and Herr Brandtner had also returned and settled down once again to his grocer's routine. How I envied Ulli, Heidi and Lieselotte, all reunited with their fathers. This was my seventh Christmas without Papa, who was still in that awful POW camp in Pisa. It seemed so very unfair.

My Christmas presents that year included two beautiful sweaters Mama had knitted from Aunt Herma's designs. One was royal blue with a red-and-white toadstool border, the other in shades of green, brown and orange featured grazing deer among autumn leaves and wild mushrooms. I could hardly wait to show off my new jumpers to my school-friends. But how would the nuns react to Omi's present, the dainty gold ring with the red stone? Concerning jewellery the convent motto had always been:

Die Jugend schmückt sich selbst,
Das Alter muss sich zieren!
(Youth will adorn itself,
Only age needs decoration).

In the end nobody objected to the little ruby ring on my finger and every time I looked at it I thought of Omi.

'Miracles never cease,' Mama had exclaimed over my keenness to sort out my toy cupboard; and little Christa, the convent's latest addition, had hopped with delight over her 'new' dolls and books. Generally, only pupils of secondary school age were accepted as boarders but Christa was 'our special case'. Since the divorce of her Viennese parents she had lived with a Zwettl relation and attended school at the convent. When her aunt fell seriously ill the six-year-old became a full boarder and my little charge. I had to help Christa with washing and dressing, supervise her at dinner and check her homework every day. We became very attached to each other and, almost fifty years later, are still in touch.

EIGHTEEN

A STRANGER CALLED PAPA

One day in early 1947 there was a knock on our classroom door.

'Can Jutta Schweighofer come to the reception? It's urgent,' I heard Sister Imelda say. My class teacher seemed not too pleased but agreed to let me go.

'Hurry up, dear, you've got a very important visitor,' Sister Imelda smiled but wouldn't reveal his identity. Who could it be? He had to be very special indeed to justify my being called from lessons. Taking two steps at a time I arrived breathlessly at the reception room. Through the frosted glass door I saw the outline of a man and a woman.

'Hello, Jutta,' beamed Mama, embracing me. 'Look who I've brought to see you.' The man turned. His shoulders, hunched under far too big an overcoat, straightened. A smile lit up a haggard face showing a familiar set of splendid teeth. One or two wavering steps and there I was in my father's arms, laughing and crying. For a while nobody spoke, then, suddenly, we all talked together. I heard of Papa's release from the POW camp, unforeseen even by Mama, and his surprise arrival at home after a marathon trek across the snowbound Italian mountains.

During the Easter holidays I learned about the horrors of a prison camp, 19 months of hell, as Papa described it: the nights under canvas, three men to a tent designed for two only, the diet of bread and a brew of dried fruit, the shots from the watch tower if an inmate approached the perimeter fence, the months of enforced idleness, followed by slave labour in the Italian forests . . . But it was very seldom that my father would talk of the troubles behind him; most of the time he sat brooding in silent depression or flew into a rage over the most trivial things. Those sudden outburst were really frightening and Mama's tears over Papa's discontent deeply upset me. 'Why couldn't he be happy now he was back home with his loved ones?

One day Omi took me aside and tried to explain.

'Look, darling,' she said. 'We all realise that your Papa isn't the man we've known and loved. You see, for him a world has collapsed and he can't cope. He gave the best years of his life fighting for the good of the fatherland and in the end it was all for nothing. His hero, the Führer, welcomed into Austria as our saviour, turned into a deranged maniac, responsible for the death of millions, and our economy is now worse than on the day of the Anschluss. I've known your dad for a very long time. It was back in 1927 when your Mama, who then lived with me in Vienna, first introduced us. I immediately took to the charming young man with the winning smile and my kind of humour.

He had me in stitches describing the way the young couple had met, literally bumping into each other: A student of structural engineering, Ernst had taken a holiday job with a Rastenfeld builder (Yes, you guessed correctly, it was Opa). One day while crossing the yard with a heavy sack of cement, not looking where he was going, Ernst had collided with a young lady who, to his embarrassment, turned out to be his employer's daughter. Red in the face, he introduced himself, apologising for being so clumsy.

Their following chat came to an abrupt end when 'The Boss' himself appeared on the scene. Under her father's glance of disapproval Minna hurried back to the house while Ernst picked up his sack and continued on his way across the yard. They didn't meet again before Minna's return to Vienna. Yet over the following weeks on the building site far from the city Ernst couldn't stop thinking of a certain dark-haired young lady with high cheek-bones and beautiful green eyes . . .

Back at his Viennese college with a little money in his pocket he decided he was in desperate need of new shoes. He positioned himself at Friedemann's in Mariahilfer Strasse waiting patiently till at last his chosen assistant was free. An hour later he'd finally left the store, his purchase under his arm and a triumphant smile on his face. While trying on two dozen pairs of shoes he'd exchanged addresses with his lovely assistant and arranged to meet her the following day.'

'That was the start of your parents' courtship,' my grandma summed up. 'And what happened then? Please, Omi, tell me!' I couldn't get enough of romantic tales.

'Minna's boy-friend joined our circle of friends for parties and outings and over the years I saw a lot of him,' Omi continued. 'I liked Ernst. The only quarrels we had were over politics. I worried over his growing interest in Hitler's German National Socialist Party whose radical ideas spread fast over the Austrian border and found massive support particularly among Vienna's students. You see, times were hard in the 1920s and it was a fact that Hitler had worked wonders for the German economy. In Ernst's view there was only one way of beating the recession, inflation and high unemployment in our country: to make it part of a strong German Reich. But for me who had gone through the break-up of the powerful Austrian monarchy the loss of freedom and independence of our homeland, however small at the time, was far too high a price to pay for the paradise promised by Adolf Hitler.'

'But things did improve under the Führer, didn't they, Omi?'

'For a while, dear. You see, in the long run wars never solve or improve anything; we should have learned that from past experience. But back to your Papa and his political beliefs. As much as he admired the Führer's economic miracle, he did not approve of the growing hate campaign against the Jews. We knew from our own Jewish friends and family – my nephew Franz had a Jewish wife – that they weren't all grasping, self-indulgent monsters as Nazi propaganda claimed. Many Austrian Jews, including Franz and Ruth and Friedemanns, your Mama's employers, emigrated to England or America soon after the Anschluss. Those who stayed, rich or poor, would end up in concentration camps where they suffered torture and death just for the "crime" of being Jewish.'

Seeing the horror her account of Nazi atrocities had evoked in me Omi paused and gave me a comforting hug.

'But you mustn't think that all members of the Nazi Party were evil-minded, least of all Papa. And your Mama wasn't at all interested in politics; she always hated the political arguments I had with her fiancé. But she loved Papa and admired him for standing up for his convictions. Unfortunately, Minna and Ernst could enjoy only six years of married life together, then war broke out and Papa was called up. It's up to us now,' Omi concluded, 'to help your dad recover from what he's been through over the years and make him face normal life again.'

But normal life for my father meant getting back to his job, which at the time was out of the question. It wasn't through lack of business; construction work had been neglected during the war and builders' skills were badly needed. Yet, as a former party member, Papa was banned from running a business. In the end Mama could stand it no longer and decided she had to do something about the desperate situation. Unknown to Papa she called at the county council offices in Krems, where the cases of former Nazis were being reviewed. Insisting on seeing the Bezirkshauptmann (council chief) in person, she bravely presented the case of her husband. Unlike the big Nazis at the Nuremberg Trials, Papa was neither a war criminal nor a party profiteer, she argued; through seven-and-a-half years of military service and captivity he had already paid dearly for his convictions. Was it fair to punish a desperate man further and deprive him of earning a living for 'himself and his family'? Mama's plea proved successful and Papa's business licence was restored within weeks.

In late 1947 my dad started building again. But, like his father and father-in-law after World War One, he had to start from scratch. The war had claimed several of his men, others had found different employment, and the only means of transport Papa had was a second-hand bicycle. There was also a severe shortage of building materials but the farmers' ingenuity soon overcame that. They took their horses and carts to the no-man's land down the road and, under the noses of Russian soldiers, dismantled the Döllersheim ruins brick by brick. Cleaned up, these materials were now fit for re-use.

As soon as Papa could afford a small motor-cycle his building radius could be extended beyond the Rastenfeld area. This meant employing more bricklayers and training new apprentices. Success in business worked wonders for my dad's confidence and, gradually, he became his old self again. With the office in Mama's capable hands, the Schweighofer's building firm thrived once more.

The year 1947 was memorable to us in several ways.

Uncle Karl's marriage at 41 delighted the whole family. His bride, Poldi, a farmer's daughter from a neighbouring village, and his brother Willi's class-mate, was 16 years his junior.

For me a family wedding meant great excitement. With clothes still on ration I couldn't have a bridesmaid's dress but still felt very special in my Sunday best and my only pair of lace-up boots. The long wedding poem I recited for the bride and groom went down well with everyone at the village church.

The reception venue was Schweighofer's in Friedersbach – where else? and Grandmother and Uncle Karl had excelled in catering for their own family wedding. The buffet's volume and variety proved quite overwhelming for someone like me, used to a meagre boarding school diet. One gateau which really intrigued me had the shape of a cabbage with green marzipan leaves and edible caterpillars.

'You must ask Jutta for a dance,' my new aunt's youngest brother, sixteen-year-old Hermann, was urged but he flatly refused. I didn't hold it against him; at twelve-and-a-half I felt much happier in the company of older men. The celebrations continued until the early hours but for me it was back to boarding-school.

The next family reception followed the christening of Karl Schweighofer junior. Now I had three 'real' cousins, all of them boys. How delighted I was when several months later a daughter arrived at my youngest uncle's home. Under Sister Imelda's guidance I crocheted a complete baby outfit in delicate pink but never saw my youngest cousin wear it. It wasn't until 1950 that Willi dared venture into the Russian sector to introduce his wife, Ida, and daughter, Silvia, to the family.

There was a definite generation gap between Grandmother and Auntie Poldi, obvious even to a thirteen-year-old. I found it strange that my new aunt kept using the formal 'Sie' every time she addressed her mother-in-law. And despite trying her best, the young woman could never match the calibre, experience and sheer single-mindedness of the older one.

My grandparents' formal retirement in 1948 changed little in the relationship between Grandmother and Auntie Poldi. Retired or not, Frau Schweighofer senior always appeared to be in charge. Uncle Karl, though easy-going like his father, was very much his own boss. Shrewd and hardworking, he soon developed ideas of his own to further his business. He let the farm, concentrating on the pub, restaurant and butchery trade, and began to modernise and expand. He had the kitchen refurbished and a retirement flat for his parents built across the yard. The first-floor dance hall was converted into guest rooms and a large, modern replacement built at the rear of the house. The one to carry out these ambitious projects was, of course, Papa.

Our house, too, underwent changes beyond recognition. You now entered through a much wider doorway at the far end of the building. The original vaulted entrance was turned into a cosy living-room flanked by a new office and the master bedroom. The days of domestic servants long gone and Papa could see no point in keeping a maid's room. He incorporated it in the kitchen, which now had access to the yard. And, last, not least, the mini-flat was converted into a bedroom for me, a modern bathroom and W.C. It seemed that every time I arrived home from boarding school there was yet another surprise waiting. But with my parents so involved in the business less and less time could be spared for family life. So during the school holidays I practically lived in the granny-flat. Omi always had time for me and the little problems I experienced in growing up.

In 1949, reaching the end of compulsory education, I had to make plans for my future career.

No longer were daughters of middle-class families destined for marriage, motherhood and household only; post-war experiences had changed attitudes. But my parents still hoped that one day I would follow into Mama's footsteps.

'Why don't you go in for business studies and domestic science?' they advised. But my plans were entirely different.

'You know I'm not interested in business,' I snapped at Mama, 'and why should I want to learn about the boring old household chores you're making me do anyway?'

My parents puzzled over who was responsible for my sudden interest in teaching – surely not Frau Hartmann or Frau Glatz?

Was it the example of relatives in the profession or the encouragement of the nuns? My friend Inge's decision to train as a teacher certainly influenced my own career plans. Besides, I liked the idea of a vocational college with Matura (A-levels) and the option of university entrance. The nearest training college and therefore my first choice was the 'Convent of the English Ladies' in Krems, the same institute Omi had attended some fifty years previously.

The nuns' reputation of being strict and selective did not put me off; it only made me work harder for the entrance exam.

'I'll buy you a really good fountain pen if you pass,' promised Papa, 'but if you don't you can have two.' I passed and made do with one pen.

NINETEEN

THE COLLEGE OF THE ENGLISH LADIES

The important exam day had not got off to a very good start.

To reach Krems on the Danube, 36 kilometres south-east from Rastenfeld, before 8 am, Mama and I had to catch the 5.30 service bus. An hour and dozens of stops later we'd reached the spot where the Waldviertel plateau drops sharply to the valley of the river Krems. As soon as the driver began to negotiate the numerous hair-pin bends the dreaded travel sickness once again overwhelmed me. Would this awful journey ever end?

'Come on, dear, we have arrived!' Mama's voice shook me out of my

Krems, with the parish church (r) and the Piaristen Church (l).

Krems – The 'Sie-Mandl' fountain.

The Institute B.M.V. in Krems.

misery. The stop was Wiener Brücke, the bridge over the Krems river on the outskirts of the town.

Pale and disorientated, I followed my mother along the route which was to become so familiar over the following years: first along the top end of Landstrasse, the town's main shopping street, then, turning sharp right and up the cobbled incline of the Hoher Markt.

'Have a look at this, Jutta!' Mama stopped at an ornate fountain at the bottom of the hill. Still queasy, I made myself focus on the well-known landmark of medieval Krems. Two stone figures dominated the 'Sie-Mandl' fountain: a knight kneeling before his dame who, hands on hips, stands menacingly over him. The humour of this sign of early feminism and the long haul up the Hoher Markt finally rid me of the wretched travel sickness. An imposing fortress-like building rose from the hilltop. I had reached my destination.

Walking through the college's main entrance I noticed the words 'Institut B.M.V.' over the ornate, wood-carved door. 'Beatae Mariae Virginis' (Of the Blessed Virgin Mary), I learned later, was the Latin name of the order of nuns, commonly known as 'Englische Fräulein' after their English founder, Mary Ward.

Compared with my previous convent school, the college I entered in September 1949 seemed enormous and very different. The only teachers' training college for girls in the region, it also offered a three years' course for Domestic Science and boarding facilities for several hundred students. Included were also a Kindergarten and primary school, essential for the student teachers' educational practice. I was surprised to find definite class distinction among the 'English Ladies'. An air of superiority about them, the professionals were addressed 'Mater' while we called the more modestly attired domestic staff 'Soror' (Sister).

Not all our tutors were nuns. The college employed a number of female lay teachers and even men from the training college for boys. My heart-throb was our English tutor, Professor Mittermeyer, alias 'Lord'. The sonorous voice of the small, grey-suited man reciting Hamlet or a speech by President Lincoln would turn my legs to jelly every time. This teenage crush on 'Lord' was probably the extension of my deep love for the subject he taught.

Our chaplain and R.E. teacher, Professor Eigenbauer, irreverently called 'Eix', was liked by all the girls. He often talked about the war and how his experiences as a Luftwaffe fighter pilot had made him enter the priesthood rather late in life. Our verdict of 'Eix': a sincere, easily approachable man of the world in a dog collar.

All male tutors, except Eix, would address us politely with 'Fräulein' and 'Sie'. We, in turn, behaved in a most lady-like manner during their lessons and worked hard to gain their approval. The result was generally good marks in the subjects taught by men. I must admit that our behaviour was not as impeccable towards some lady teachers.

Hardly as 'beneficial' as her name suggested, Dr. Heilsam, our young and inexperienced Latin tutor, was top of the unpopularity list. The personality clashes between Dr. Heilsam and us often led to the intervention of Mater Wieninger, the college principal. Mater Wieninger also taught Mathematics, after Latin the most likely stumbling block. I, for one, had to work hard to gain reasonable marks in the subject which never was my strongest point. Although cool and aloof, Mater Wieninger was a fair teacher and widely respected by staff and pupils. Not as crucial as Maths and Latin, but even more disliked, was Russian. No one could see the logic of learning the hated language just because we lived in the Russian zone. Professor Schalek, a sweet, silver-haired lady of Czech origin, appreciated the prejudice against her subject but had to keep up appearances when the Commandant came to inspect classes.

'You, too, my son Brutus?' I remember her sighing when I was once caught cheating during a written exam. But most of the time she turned a blind eye, handing out better marks than we deserved. Consequently, we had little knowledge of a language studied over a period of two years.

My favourite science, Natural History, comprising Zoology, Botany, Geology and Human Biology, was taught by our form mistress, Mater Hofer. I wasn't too keen on her other subject, Geography, or the gruelling mountain treks she loved to engage in. I liked art, but not the art teacher, Mater Wansch, who was cross-eyed and totally lacked finesse. Neither Inge nor I, considered the best in art, ever received praise from Mater Wansch. In contrast, Mater Ehrhart, the elocution teacher, was very refined. Yet her subject was never taken seriously by most of her students. Why should we sacrifice our regional accents for the 'cultured voice of the ideal teacher'? I also begrudged the amount of time spent on sport, the subject which has always been my Achilles heel. I had nothing against Professor Pfeiler, our young P.E. mistress; what I didn't like was the frustration and sense of failure I always associated with P.E.

The climate of the Danube valley took some getting used to. Those of us from the Waldviertel, unfamiliar with the sultry summers in Krems, often sought refuge in the convent garden. This was a pleasant spot bordering the city wall, with views over the river Krems and far beyond. To prevent their charges from sitting on the parapet, day-dreaming instead of studying, the nuns had taken precautions. Thousands of spikes of jagged glass also proved an effective deterrent for young, foolish 'knights', hell-bent on reaching the 'damsels in distress' behind the wall. Contact with the opposite sex was definitely discouraged and venturing beyond the convent boundaries strictly limited.

'Make sure you're back by 5.30 sharp!' Mater Präfektin would insist, entering the purpose of our 'outing' in her registration book.

For the older girls this 'restriction of personal freedom' was a constant source of complaint but Inge and I, used to the strict discipline of convent

'The Wall' which separated the inhabitants of the Institute B.M.V. from the outside world. In the background the 'Pulverturm', a medieval gun-powder magazine.

Krems – (l to r): The College of the English Ladies (back); parish church; tower in the medieval wall (gun-powder magazine); Piaristen Church.

schools, found life in Krems comparatively easy. Although meals were not much better than in Zwettl, nobody forced us to eat what we didn't like. And, to avoid going hungry, we could always draw on the provisions brought back from home.

It was those regular weekends at home that I regarded as the greatest privilege of all. Not that I saw a lot of my parents. Their Saturdays would be spent in the office paying out wages and organising work for the coming week and Sunday mornings were reserved for consultations with clients. But there was always dear Omi in her favourite place by the wireless, eagerly waiting for her granddaughter's latest tales about her old college.

'Will you check the laundry basket and see what needs mending before you start ironing, dear,' Mama's voice would call from the office as soon as I'd set foot in the house. But a little housework was a small price to pay for such treats as my mother's home cooking, an express laundry service and a leisurely soak in the bath. Besides, domestic chores were now so much easier since Papa bought an electric cooker, refrigerator and washing-machine. With my batteries recharged after the weekend at home, I would happily face the studies ahead, even the ordeal of the 5 am bus.

'Hey, what's this? Not all top marks like in Zwettl?' Papa teased, studying my first college report.

'You don't know how hard school is in Krems,' was my immediate defence. 'Nearly everyone has a Four in Maths and Latin. At least, I didn't get a Five.'

Tough measures had been taken to reduce the original intake of students by a quarter to 30. Among the 'survivors' were Inge and two more girls from the Gymnasium Zwettl: Helga Weinberger, the school-inspector's daughter, and Irmgard Wandl, whose father managed the agricultural college Edelhof. Irmi soon became another best friend and our trio (Inge, Irmi and I) often visited one another's homes. Blue-eyed, blonde-plaited Irmi sometimes rebelled against 'petty' boarding-school rules.

'I really don't know how you put up with a girdle,' she'd grumble, and carry on wearing knee socks instead of stockings.

'All your Two's could be One's,' Mater Hofer kept moaning at one of her brightest pupils, 'if only you'd try that bit harder.'

She was probably right, and Irmi's refusal to take notes for revision was partly to blame. But my friend's worst breach of convent rules happened one winter's night when, as usual, we shivered in our icy bedrooms under the roof.

'I've had enough of cold feet and frost bite,' Irmi said. 'Let's have a proper fire for once.' Having requisitioned a box of coal from the depot, she and two other brave souls kept feeding the iron stove till it glowed red.

But our euphoria over a warm bedroom soon ended as the nun on night duty promptly reported her findings to Mater Superior. The next morning the case of the girls who 'stooped so low as to steal' was brought in front of the chaplain. Listening to our side of the story dear Eix decided we'd been 'within our moral rights' and had 'acted in self-defence only'. The fuel thief incident was never mentioned again.

As much as I liked Irmi, sharing a bedroom with her had a drawback; she snored. Fed up with having to get out of bed to shake her, I came up with an ingenious device: a piece of string, threaded through Irmi's eiderdown cover, leading to my own bedside table. It worked like a dream. One tug and the infuriating noise stopped. But, getting wiser and increasingly colder, my friend kept hanging on to her duvet. The result: a torn button-hole. That was the first and only occasion in our five years together that Irmi and I really fell out.

Another girl who had survived the first year's 'weeding-out process' was Loisi Galler. The fact that her uncle, Leopold Figl, was Chancellor of Austria at the time meant no great deal. What did impress us about Loisi was her sheer size. The tallest in class, she always headed our P.E. line-up, with Irmi, Helga and me somewhere in the middle and tiny Inge a frustrated last. Loisi's stature and confidence combined with a rare organisational talent made her the ideal class representative. Thirty-odd years after leaving college she is still in touch with all classmates and arranges regular reunions, with attendances averaging 90%. Fluent in English after many visits to Britain, she has organised numerous holiday exchanges, especially for her own children. Tragically widowed, the grandmother of four is now a regular volunteer worker at the Austrian Hospice in Jerusalem.

The intensive studies at college had put extra strain on my deteriorating eyesight.

'I know just the man to get to the bottom of this,' said Omi and took me to the Viennese specialist who had monitored her own eyes for 40-odd years.

At the end of a thorough examination Professor Guist explained the term 'astigmatism' to me and made out a prescription for new lenses.

'To prevent further deterioration I advise you to avoid bending and lifting, indeed any strain on your stomach muscles,' he said. And, thinking of the dreaded P.E. lessons, I happily promised to comply. But then came the blow:

'You also must wear your spectacles constantly,' Professor Guist added in a stern voice.

I was devastated. Sixteen-years-of-age, I had become very conscious of my appearance.

After shedding several pounds of 'puppy fat' I had finally had my hair cut and permed. And Papa, delighted with his daughter's new grown-up look, had bought me a stylish cornflower-blue coat and light-grey fashion boots which I wore with great pride. Now the rotten glasses would spoil everything. Recalling the taunts of the boys at junior school I was quite convinced that no man would ever find me attractive enough to ask for my hand in marriage. It didn't help that several girls in my class started boasting about their boyfriends back home, while my sole conquest was someone I only remember as 'The Russian Teacher'. Most weekends on the journey home this guy would sit next to me on the bus, chatting me up. I couldn't stand him. What girl in her right mind would fall for a male chauvinist with nothing better to do than teach Russian? But it took weeks before my admirer got the message and stopped pestering me. For once I was glad of my travel-sickness attacks which, no doubt, had helped to deter him.

Now Paul was something entirely different. I'd met this blond, bronzed hunk of a man in the summer of 1951 when swimming in the mill pond. Introducing himself as Rastenfeld's newest teacher, he'd instantly bowled me over. How flattering that such a good-looking, educated guy who was also an all-round sportsman and musician should be interested in an unsporting schoolgirl with glasses. Our age difference of eleven years seemed quite insignificant; if anything, it was an extra attraction. However, what I did find peculiar in Paul was his subservience to his widowed mother with whom he shared a house in the village. Whenever we met, Frau Felsinger seemed to be present, dominating the conversation and generally taking over. Paul and I had dated for a few weeks when his Viennese brother and sister-in-law asked us to join them in a family trip to Venice. Of course, Mother would come, too, they assured my concerned parents. I was excited! This was my first journey abroad, and God knows what might happen between Paul and me in such a romantic setting. But nothing happened at all. Five glorious days in Venice and Paul still addressed me with 'Sie'. Back home he missed a date with the silliest excuse ('I had to take Mother to the shoemaker in the next village'). That did it! It was the end of a relationship that never really got off the ground.

There wasn't much time for boyfriends during the last two college years. Preparing for the 'Matura' in five compulsory and two optional subjects made heavy demands on us. Although my academic record had steadily improved since that first mixed report – a Two in Latin meant 'tops' for a subject in which a One was unheard of – I constantly worried over Maths.

To aid the fourth- and fifth-formers' concentration a large room had been allocated to us. But most evenings this private study was converted into a 'dance hall'. Practising our self-taught steps to popular records would help us unwind after the intense swatting of the day. Refusing permission for a mixed dance course at the male training college, the nuns had suggested all-female tuition at the convent instead. Unanimously, we'd turned down this offer and proved we could manage without.

My parents began to worry over the effect the general 'alienation from the real world' might have on their daughter.

'Why not go external?' Mama suggested one weekend when Inge and Irmi had come home with me.

'Great idea!' was their immediate response and, with the blessing of three sets of parents, the inseparable trio began the hunt for a flat. Unfortunately, there was very little property suitable for the needs of three final-year students. Disillusioned, we abandoned our plans of independence and put up with 'institutional life' for several more months. Admittedly, fourth- and fifth-formers enjoyed many privileges denied to the younger pupils. In groups of three or four we could attend productions of visiting theatre troops as well as approved films at the local cinemas. For art classes we frequently ventured into the Old Town to catch its charm on paper and canvas. Following our teacher's preference for the boys' labs. we were even trusted to take our Physics lessons at the male training college. And, in addition to educational outings further afield, there were leisurely trips to the tourist paradise of the 'Wachau'. Tracing the route of the Nibelungs along the Danube's most scenic part you would come across quaint villages with castles and monasteries surrounded by vineyards and orchards.

We heard of Aggstein's 'Robber Barons' wicked practice of intercepting merchant ships on the Danube and the detainment and torture of their crew. Shuddering, we viewed the castle's infamous 'Rose Garden', a tiny platform, with a sheer drop to the river. From here, the saga goes, desperate prisoners would rather jump to their deaths than slowly die of starvation. Less macabre tales surround the castle of Dürnstein, where Richard the Lionheart was held prisoner by Leopold of Austria, his rival crusader. Tracked down by his minstrel, Blondel, King Richard was eventually

Dürnstein Castle (where Richard the Lionheart was imprisoned) above the village of the same name, and the Danube.

Stift Zwell, Cistercian Monastery, aerial view.

returned to his homeland. They said the ransom paid for him was high enough to build an entire new city. Located south of Vienna, it was named Wiener Neustadt. Although not as famous as the Wachau, the Krems valley, too, exuberates in castles and vineyards. We got to know this area well when our teaching practice was extended to the primary school of Rehberg.

However, the best practical experience was the 'Waldviertel country school week' in the spring of 1953. Helga, Irmi, Inge and I specially looked forward to show off our home area, particularly Stift Zwettl, to our classmates. Only a stone's-throw from the town of the same name, the monastery is situated in a meander of the Kamp and surrounded by dense forests. Founded and still inhabited by Cistercian monks, the complex comprises various styles from austere Romanesque beginnings to the Baroque splendour, so typical of Austrian church architecture. According to legend, the monastery's site was determined by an apparition of Our Lady guiding the monks to an oak in full leaf in the deepest winter. The wood-carving of a green oak tree on the church's high altar reminds the congregation of this founder legend.

The sight of 30 young ladies in a monks' domain caused quite a stir among the locals. Farmers, going about their early business, would stare in amazement as groups of girl cyclists emerged from behind the monastery walls, bound for the neighbouring schools. And most of Stift Zwettl's village population lined the street, shaking their heads when, often soaked to the skin, we returned to our monastic quarters. April 1953 was a very wet month!

The experience of one rainy morning can still send shivers up my spine: Millions of earthworms from infantile pink to the mature brown of the species had covered the roads. Stretched out motionless, they seemed to revel in the god-send of dampness, totally blind to the acute dangers around them. Trying to dodge them was futile and thousands of worms must have perished that morning, squashed under our bicycle wheels.

I have another recollection of our week in Stift Zwettl, an embarrassing moment for the girls involved. One night saw Kathi and Emma, in their night-dresses, dash red-faced through our dormitory door.

'Guess where we've just been?' they spluttered. 'Not to the wash-room but to the monks' evening assembly!' Another prank of those mischievous choir boys! Apparently, they'd switched all the signs on the identical doors of the corridor.

Soon the Stift Zwettl country school week was a memory only as, back at college, we braced ourselves for the end spurt. Once again, it was 'all work and no play'. Unlike other A-level students, convent girls weren't allowed a 'Matura-Ball'. A 'Matura-Reise' (outing of the whole A-level year, often abroad) was equally out of the question.

But we were adamant to produce a 'Matura-Zeitung', the traditional satirical A-level magazine. It was to be of outstanding brilliance. Its title: *'Bunte Steine'* (Colourful Stones) after A. Stifter's collection of short stories, each stone representing a member of staff.

Those good at poetry, especially Inge, would spend half the right in the W.C., where peace and torchlight sustained inspiration. Inge also drew cartoons of distinctly featured tutors, while the cover illustration, an untidy stone heap with weeds growing from it, was provided by me. The magazine was just about ready for printing when our secret leaked out. Summoned to Mater Wieninger's office, we thought the whole enterprise doomed. But we had misjudged our Principal as lacking in humour (as 'The Diamond' she'd come out rather well!). After a slight dressing-down we had official permission to publish the – uncensored – 'Stones'. Distribution, of course, had to wait until after the exams.

The written Matura in May 1954, lasting four days for as many subjects, proved not too much of a trauma. Every morning the invigilators, all college staff, would break the seals of the official envelopes and hand out the papers. We then had four hours to solve them. Due to strict security measures cheating was virtually impossible. Even leaving the exam room for 'spending a penny' entailed the most thorough search. With subject tutors acting as

Matura at the College of the English Ladies in Krems (May 1954).

First row from left: 1st, Mater Wansch; 3rd, M. Marckgott; 5th, M. Wieninger (Principal); 7th, M. Hofer; 8th, Dr. Lang; 9th, Prof. Eigenbauer.
Second row from left: 1st, Prof. Zillinger; 2nd Helga; 8th, Prof. Mittermeyer; 9th, Prof. Wolter.
Third row from left: 6th, Myself (with glasses); 7th, Irmi; 11th, Loisi (behind Prof. Mittermeyer).
Top row from left: 8th, Inge.

internal examiners, the results of written papers were known within days. As expected, I'd done well in English and Latin but my 'substandard' German essay had been marked with a sorry Three. However, the biggest surprise was to come with my Maths paper.

'Congratulations, Jutta! You've done exceptionally well,' smiled an amazed Mater Wieninger. And there it was, in black and white, the incredible grade One! Our tutors' marks had yet to be approved by the Education Authority's representative, who was also acting chairman for the oral exams. This was Dr. Käfer, school inspector in charge of Lower Austria and, according to Helga's father, a hard, unapproachable man.

With the day of the orals looming, my nerves started to fray.

'I'll be all right in Natural History and Pedagogics,' I kept telling myself, 'but why did I ever agree to switch from English to German?'

In obligatory 'Matura Black' I stood waiting at the examination hall entrance blaming my initial 'S', so late in the alphabet, for the nerve-wracking delay.

'Phew! Am I glad that's over!' Elfi Riepl emerged with a relieved grin. 'Your turn next, Jutta; I wish you good luck! By the way, his name fits our chairman.

Taking my seat opposite Dr. Käfer I realised what she meant. With his round, dark-suited shoulders, his magnified bespectacled eyes and rasping voice he really resembled a beetle. The comparison, like a tonic, helped calm my nerves. Despite frequent interruptions of the 'Beetle' I excelled in my orals. The result in German Literature had more than compensated for my poor essay. Alas, two other examinees had not been successful and faced re-sits later that year. The 'White Flag' for a 100% pass-rate had escaped the 'English Ladies' yet again.

'Hallo! I've got brilliant news!' Mama, waiting anxiously for that crucial telephone call, could tell from my voice I had passed. What made my family still happier was my pass with distinction.

'I knew you would do it!' A very proud Papa had left work early to pick up his daughter. The time had arrived to say goodbye to my teachers and friends at the convent.

'We had some good years together,' I pondered and promised: 'See you all sometime in the future!'

'I do love the beetle, Papa.' Grinning, I climbed into my father's brand-new V.W ... 'Looks much more fun than the specimen we had to suffer this morning!' And as the car door shut firmly behind me I watched another door closing on a very important part of my life.

TWENTY

FILLING THE GAP

1954 was not the best year for newly fledged primary school teachers. The vacancies arising through the dismissal or early retirement of Nazis in the profession had long been filled and far too many new graduates were chasing the few available posts. One of hundreds, my name had been added to the local Education Authority's register and I braced myself for a long wait.

'What chance is there for us ordinary mortals,' was Inge's comment, 'when not even the school inspector's daughter can get a decent job in teaching?' Convent educated Helga, at barely twenty, had taken the position of governess at a home for delinquent teenage girls. To me, Inge herself showed just as much courage by accepting a teaching post high up in the Tyrolean Alps. But her letters portraying life at a tiny, isolated mountain school were always written with great humour. There wasn't much mail from Irmi; she'd always been a lazy correspondent. But I knew from her parents that she and Loisi were doing au pair work in Britain. While Irmi had struck it lucky with her employer, the Liberal leader, Jo Grimond, Loisi found herself in a dire situation. Alone all day with three mentally handicapped children, she hadn't much chance to improve her English. Though her second au pair job proved slightly better, Loisi left Britain for West Germany and a teaching post in Hamburg.

I was undecided about my own future. Desperate for a job in education, I felt unable to work under conditions like Helga's, Inge's or Loisi's. Nor could I see myself as a bank, post office or local government clerk like other classmates. But how beneficially to fill the months – or years – till my name had reached the top of the list for 'teachers in waiting'?

'Why not spend some time at home?' Mama suggested. 'Papa and I could do with a little help in the office.'

I hadn't the heart to express my dislike of clerical work yet again. Perhaps this was the chance to repay my hardworking parents for eight years of expensive boarding-school education?

'All right,' I agreed. 'I'll stay for a year,' and within days was a registered employee of Schweighofer's building firm.

'I would recommend you have your daughter's coming of age brought forward,' the accountant advised. 'Considerable tax benefits could be gained that way.'

So I was whisked to the solicitor's office and confronted with questions like: 'Can you tell me the difference between a foal and a pony?' and 'What causes day and night?'

Listening in, Papa just couldn't resist mentioning my A-level pass with distinction. That seemed to satisfy the official that I had reached the maturity and intelligence of the average 21-year-old. He signed the document, Papa and I countersigned, and my premature coming of age was confirmed.

'But I have to advise you of certain rights your daughter may exercise from this day,' the clerk warned my father. 'Marriage without parental consent is one of those prerogatives.' But as, to his knowledge, nobody was waiting in the wings to sweep his daughter off her feet, Papa was prepared to take that risk.

Work didn't start immediately, though.

'Don't you think that after all that swatting Jutta deserves a little holiday?' Mama appealed to Papa's conscience. 'The Boss' complied under one condition: I had to register for a typing course at a Krems Secretarial school.

'Done!' I agreed and took myself off to Uncle Joschi's abode in 'Green Styria'.

The train journey south came to a sudden end at Mitterbach village.

'You have now reached the demarcation line between the Soviet and British zones of occupation!' the loudspeaker hailed. 'No passengers allowed off the train! Remain seated and have your identification papers ready!'

Peering through the window I found the platform crawling with uniformed Russians. One by one they boarded the train. Everybody searched nervously for their identification card, a document in four languages every Austrian had to carry. Checking the cover photograph against my anxious face, the investigator returned my card without comment. Unlike some of my fellow passengers I did not even have to open my suitcase. After a good half hour's inspection the officials seemed satisfied. The Russian sentry on the platform waved his rifle and the train was allowed to proceed. The whole operation had somewhat unnerved me. At home things had settled down by now and the Russians were keeping a low profile. I was not prepared for such a concentrated presence of the occupying force nine years after the war.

The tranquillity of Styria, the county across the demarcation line, soon made me relax. Passing my eyes were vast evergreen forests and lush meadows strewn with alpine roses and gentians. There was the sound of cow bells echoing from hill-side pastures – and not one foreign soldier in sight. The mountains enclosed Uncle Joschi's chalet; you could almost touch one craggy, grey giant from his balcony. I couldn't help thinking how well my uncle had done for himself since leaving Rastenfeld. Still connected with his beloved forests, he now managed a small factory which turned wood pulp into high quality paper. The whole of Styria seemed to breathe an air of prosperity still missing in my own home province. Heidi, a bubbly 13-year-old, and her parents made me very welcome indeed. We had a splendid time swimming and rowing in the nearby Lake Lunz, and climbing up to an 'Alm', the 'summer resort for our cows', as Heidi put it. We also enjoyed visits to Styria's capital, Graz, and the most famous Austrian shrine, Mariazell. I enquired about Heidi's aunt, with whom we'd lost touch since her departure.

'Herma has made her home in Vienna,' Aunt Milli replied. 'Enjoys her work in interior design and the love of an adoring husband. But she still suffers from nerves, can't seem to put the past behind her . . .'

Arriving at home after my Styrian fortnight I was surprised to find my holiday further extended.

'Remember Friedl, Friedl Trappl?' Mama introduced our latest guest. She's come for a summer break in the country. I hope you two girls will enjoy your time together.'

Friedl, the little daughter of Papa's Viennese cousin, had grown into a stunning young lady who looked as if she'd just stepped out of a fashion magazine. I was soon to discover two more of her enviable features: she could develop a gorgeous suntan in minutes and instantly attract every male in sight. Apart from that, I really liked Friedl and she seemed to enjoy her country holiday with us. Friedl played the accordion, I the guitar, and one day 'the sound of music' – or was it my pretty cousin? – lured a young stranger to our open living-room window. Tobias Zoller, an instructor for a Krems driving school, had been sent to Rastenfeld to teach the locals.

'Driving is a must for everyone nowadays,' Papa had insisted, persuading me to enrol for the course. And the charming, good-looking course leader seemed most keen to meet his prospective students.

'I'm delighted to teach an attractive young lady like you, Fräulein Jutta,' he smiled, holding my hand a fraction too long for a mere introduction. Was there a glimmer of jealousy in my cousin Friedl's flashing green eyes?

'Tough!' I thought. 'At seventeen she's still too young for driving.'

Rudi Österreicher and Herr Brandtner had also enrolled for the course but there were very few women candidates, Ilse, the daughter of our former Ortsgruppenleiter, being one of them. With the Russian commandant's office dismantled some time ago, the Heidrichs had returned from Upper Austria and again ran the family store plus the new filling-station. Tobias Zoller soon became a household name in Rastenfeld. Most evenings he lectured on mechanics and the highway code and there was daily driving practice. The school car, a VW beetle like Papa's, proved to be an advantage for me, but my charming instructor's attention seemed to go well beyond driving.

Papa began to wonder why the school car continually passed our house and all learners were made to reverse into our drive. These manoeuvres continued long after the day my pretty cousin had squeezed her hooped petticoat into the post bus and departed for home. What Papa did not know about was Tobias Zoller's habit of flirting through the mirror with his lady passengers in the back. Not that I consciously encouraged my instructor's advances; but they did add some spice to a dull exercise and turned our group lessons into exciting outings. The test itself, comprising two written papers and practical driving, was more nerve-wracking for me than the Matura. It didn't help that only days earlier Tobias Zoller had been involved in a big scandal. The whole village talked about the driving instructor's alleged affair with his landlady, followed by a punch-up with her enraged husband. Whatever his reputation, Tobias must have been pretty good at his job as 90% of his 40-odd pupils, myself included, passed at the first attempt.

Papa sometimes let me borrow the car when he didn't need it for work. But there was no question of my driving to Krems to attend the typing course there. Yet, despite the arduous bus journey, Thursday became the highlight of my week; a most welcome break from typing job estimates and

Lake Ottenstein with the castle of Lichtenfels in the foreground.

business letters and a surfeit of tedious housework. At least our weekends had become more family-orientated.

'Let's walk to Ottenstein and see what's going on there?' Papa would suggest most Sunday afternoons. The castle of Ottenstein, stripped and vandalised by the Russians but recently restored, had become the centre of a new exciting development.

A massive barrier, erected nearby, had dammed the Grosser Kamp and its tributaries and changed the familiar landscape beyond recognition. The Purzelkamp valley, incorporating the old Friedersbach road, now formed part of the vast new Ottenstein lake. Rising to the tops of the rocks and submerging the 'Herrgottstein' at the bottom, the dammed water had created a centre island around Lichtenfels castle. The heart of the Austrian Waldviertel now resembled a Norwegian fiord. Most villagers, including my father, regarded 'Project Ottenstein' with enthusiasm and wonder.

'It'll put the Waldviertel on the map,' was the general view. 'We'll get cheaper electricity and also attract tourists to our neck of the woods.'

Excursions to well-known beauty spots in the area had become a popular weekend pursuit. Often the Österreichers and Brandtners and our new friends, the Heinz family, would join us which, in my opinion, always added to the fun. Ulli Brandtner, now apprenticed to a big wholesaler in Gars/Kamp, was no longer with us, but my friendship with the Österreicher family had deepened since their three gorgeous children had come along.

It was one of those weekend excursions that set a sudden end to my short-lived driving career. A recent site accident had put Papa's left arm in plaster and me at the wheel of his car. A trip through autumn-tinged forests had led us to Friedersbach for afternoon tea at the Schweighofers' inn. Returning from there, our convoy descended the hill near Rastenberg Castle when a sudden sunburst almost blinded me.

'Mustn't hit Brandtners' car.' flashed through my mind. I panicked and instinctively pulled to the right. There was a horrible crunching noise as the VW came to a sudden halt. Dazed and bewildered, I noticed Papa's face going a very deep red. I was used to my father's short fuse but had never seen him so furious.

'You stupid girl! What d'you think you're doing? Isn't the road wide enough for you?' he blew up in front of what seemed Rastenberg's whole population. Carrying on about 'the incompetence of women drivers', he began to unwrap his dented car from milestone 25. By the time Papa had finished shouting I was in floods of tears, my confidence shattered and my mind finally made up: never again would I take the wheel of a car owned by my father.

The year I spent at home not only strengthened old friendships but also created new ones. Through Auntie Poldi we became very close with her Zwettl relatives, the Dirnbergers. A teenage accident resulting in the amputation of a leg had not stopped Sophie, Aunt Poldi's sister, from leading a normal and indeed very active life. I always admired the way this attractive, lively young woman coped cheerfully with a demanding husband, four children, a big house and a large dog and still found the time and energy to entertain a substantial circle of friends.

'Tasso is our sheep,' Sophie joked, showing off several beautiful sweaters she'd knitted for the children from the dog's wool.

It had been love at first sight between Papa and the black Alsatian-Collie cross who greeted our visits with great outbursts of joy. Papa was crazy about dogs but so far Mama had resisted his wish for a follower of Max. My poor mother didn't realise she was heading for quite a surprise.

'There's Franz Dirnberger with Tasso,' she observed, watching the two get off the bus and head for our house one day.

Unaware of the conspiracy between the Dirnbergers and Papa, Mama learned that Tasso was here to stay. Someone else not at all keen on canine intruders was our elderly cat. Mitzi's desperate offensive from the lamp on the ceiling startled Tasso. A frantic game of hide-and-seek followed. Tearing after the black-and-white flash, the dog almost dislodged our heavy tiled stove. Another wild dash for freedom and the cat had disappeared without trace.

'Come and see this, Jutta!' Mama sounded amused and relieved. After days of fruitless searching she had at last found the absentee. By the back

Papa and Tasso – 1960.

entrance, side by side, sat dog and cat, happily eating from the same bowl. A new close friendship had been forged between the proverbial enemies. It was to last until Mitzi's natural death.

We all, Mama included, became very fond of Tasso who was affectionate, intelligent and well behaved most of the time. Not a hunter like Max, he would never stray into the woods when escorting Omi and Opa on their daily afternoon walks. However, Tasso had one filthy habit: he just couldn't resist the temptation of rolling in fresh farm manure spread on the fields. Tasso loved going to work with his master, and the black dog in the beige VW beetle soon became well-known on the building sites. Papa knew that with Tasso on guard the car was quite safe, even with open windows, unlocked doors and keys in the ignition. One day a familiar sound made my father run back to his car. He found Tasso behind the steering wheel repeatedly pushing the horn with his bottom.

'You'll have to watch that dog of yours,' one of the men teased Papa.

'Next time you're late he'll drive off and leave you behind.'

In February 1955 Fritz and Sophie Dirnberger invited me to my first ball. Organised by the local branch of the reigning conservative party, the ÖVP-Ball was the highlight of Zwettl's carnival. Wearing a long, white off-the-shoulder gown I relished the grand atmosphere and the attention of the Dirnbergers' numerous friends.

'Why not come and work for me?' suggested Dr. Raimer, the head of the tax office in Zwettl, during a waltz. But I politely declined. Surely, sometime somewhere, there was a teaching post waiting, even if it meant going abroad.

There was never enough work for a country builder during the severe Waldviertel winters.

'The farmers are hibernating again,' Papa remarked, justifying a temporary close-down of the business. For me this was the perfect opportunity to pay a return visit to Friedl in Vienna. The Trappls' caretaker flat in an office block on the Kohlmarkt was most convenient for exploring the inner city on foot. The Hofburg and St. Stephen's Cathedral were just round the corner and the boulevard of the Ring only a short walk away.

'Doesn't our Steffl look splendid again?' Friedl's voice echoed the affection every Viennese has for the city's great landmark. I shared her pride. By buying several hand-glazed tiles for 'Steffl's' new roof I'd done my little bit to restore his old glory.

'You should have seen the procession when the new Pummerin arrived back in triumph,' Friedl recalled. Recast after its destruction by fire in 1945, the famous bell had tolled once again at 'Steffl's' reopening in 1952.

'It's taken nine years to rebuild the Burgtheater and the Staatsoper,' my cousin remarked as we passed the magnificent buildings on the Ring, now almost completed. 'I've heard that the grand opening is planned for the autumn.'

Friedl and I were theatre fans, and plays and operettas – several of them

– were the highlight of my Viennese break. We also liked shopping, especially for clothes, but stayed clear from exclusive Kärntnerstrasse.

'The First District is for window-shopping only,' my cousin explained, 'I'll show you where we can get value for money.'

Combing the big stores of Mariahilfer Strasse, including Mama's former place of employment, I noticed that 'Friedemann' among other Jewish names had returned to the capital. Despite the culture and opulence displayed everywhere, Vienna still had the air of an occupied city. And, yes, it was the Russians again who kept the highest profile.

'What d'you think of this then?' asked Friedl as we passed Schwarzenberg Platz, alias Stalinplatz, the heart of the Soviet sector. 'I wonder what the victor over Napoleon would say about the present view from his palace.' Towering above the square was a most hideous monument. Its concrete column, forty metres in height, was topped by the giant bronze figure of a Russian soldier, the Red Flag high in his outstretched right hand, an automatic weapon across his chest.

'My dad told me that in the summer of '45 Russian architects and civil engineers worked round the clock to build this monstrosity,' said Friedl.

'It's commemorating Vienna's liberation by the Red Army but every Viennese calls it the *Unbekannter Plünderer* (The Unknown Plunderer)'.

The Soviets had definitely outstayed their welcome. It was their demand of 'German property' that caused all the talks over Austria's freedom to fail.

'The far-reaching concessions presented by Leopold Figl have once again resulted in the familiar "*Njet*",' was yet another depressing result of the Berlin conference of February 1954. It came as an utter surprise for a resigned Austrian nation when, a year later, the 'Staatsvertrag' (State Treaty) did materialise. 15 May 1955 was the day to end a decade of military occupation and to restore the full sovereignty lost to our country seventeen years before. The signing of the State Treaty took place at Vienna's Belvedere Palace. Awarded to Prince Eugene of Savoy for his victory over the Turks 200 years ago, this was indeed the perfect venue for the latest declaration of Austrian freedom.

Glued to the radio our family lapped up the excited commentary of the day's events:

'Several thousands of ecstatic people have crowded into the Belvedere Gardens at this significant hour . . . Molotov and his contingent arrive at the palace . . . Macmillan, Dulles, Pinay and their delegations follow . . . A warm welcome by our Dr. Figl and other heads of state . . . The crowd is clapping and cheering . . . Ministers and ambassadors now take their seats at the gold and white table in the Great Marble Hall. The historic point in time is imminent . . .

'Leopold Figl, who has worked so arduously for this significant moment, appears on the balcony. A big smile on his face, he holds up a green and gold leather-bound volume . . . The crowd explodes in thundering applause as Austria's freedom is confirmed at last . . .

'One by one, the Foreign Ministers of the "Big Four" step onto the balcony. It is Molotov who gets the biggest ovation. The reason? Tremendous relief that the Russians, all 60,000 of them, will finally leave our country! There is no end to the cheering, and thousands of delirious people begin to dance in the streets . . .'

If the State Treaty meant freedom for my homeland it also imposed far-reaching obligations. To defend the new and permanent neutrality pledged by our people, Austria needed her own military force. This 'Bundesheer' consisted of mainly young conscripts who had not fought in the war. But some like Otto, Hanni Gutmann's son, decided to make the army their career. Joining the military after the Matura, he has now reached the rank of lieutenant colonel. Döllersheim, under Russian occupation for a whole decade, was now used for training our own soldiers. For the return of this area and other 'German assets' the Soviets were granted ten years' delivery of Austrian oil and other specified goods as part of substantial reparations. On 25 October 1955 the last foreign soldier left Austrian soil. The following day was declared a national holiday, the 'Day of the Austrian Flag'.

Austria's celebrations of independence included the re-openings of the Burgtheater and Opera House and the return of the Spanish Riding School to the Hofburg. Attended by illustrious national and international audiences, these memorable events were broadcast all over the world. Regrettably, I could only follow my country's freedom celebrations over the air waves as from September 1955 I was working abroad.

Wasserburg (Bavaria) – The Old Town encircled by the river Inn.

TWENTY-ONE

A TEACHER'S LOT

WASSERBURG

The white envelope arriving at our house one June day in 1955 was indistinguishable from Papa's business mail. It was the German postmark that caught my eye and, looking closer, I realised the letter was addressed to me. It read:

'Dear Fräulein Schweighofer,
Commencing September 1955 The Commercial College for Girls, Wasserburg/Inn, Upper Bavaria has a vacancy for a tutor of history and German literature and you have been nominated as a suitable candidate for this post by our sister college, the Institut B.M.V. in Krems, Lower Austria.
Should you be interested in the position we would ask for your immediate reply in order to arrange an interview as soon as possible.

Mater Vincentia Waggerl
Principal
The Commercial College for Girls
Wasserburg/Inn
West Germany.'

I couldn't believe my eyes! I'd actually been offered a job in teaching. The prospect of instructing girls aged fourteen to seventeen in German literature did not worry me, but my other subject, modern history, seemed daunting. All through my school days our history teachers had dwelled on the ancient Romans and Greeks and Medieval Europe but always stopped short of the twentieth century. Dealing with the question of two lost wars, especially in nationalistic Bavaria, could prove tricky. I would have to prepare the lessons carefully, keep a step ahead of any pupils and try not end up in deep waters. Naturally, I accepted the position, and an interview – travel expenses paid – was arranged by returned post.

As soon as the train pulled into Wasserburg station I had forgotten the tedious journey and the thorough checks on the border. Before me lay an enchanting medieval town in a unique position. Slender church spires and ornate buildings with stepped gables marked the sky-line, reflecting in the Inn, whose meander almost enclosed the Old Town. I stopped at the bridge near the city gate admiring the delightful view, then, following the directions of a friendly, portly passer-by, began to make my way to the college B.M.V. Staggering along on heels ill-suited to Wasserburg's cobbled streets, I was quite relieved when my destination came in sight. A coat of arms incorporating the blue-and-white chequered Bavarian flag marked the old convent as a listed building. It was much smaller than its Austrian sister-college but, once inside, I found it strangely familiar. The interview consisted of an informal chat with the principal and a guided tour through the college. I was advised of the responsibilities involved and offered a very generous salary, including full board and lodgings. Invited by the nuns to stay overnight I returned home in very high spirits.

September 1955 signalled the start of two more convent years for me, only my status had changed. I was now the German and history teacher of girls not much younger than myself, and the class tutor of One A with 40 pupils. The rest of the staff consisted of elderly nuns and two middle-aged lay teachers, Frau Professor Schreiber for English and Fräulein Öhlert for P.E. Addressed as 'Fräulein Jutta' by everyone at the college, I enjoyed the best of relations with colleagues and students right from the start. Though from a different country, I never felt a stranger in Bavaria. South Germans and Austrians have much in common and the same 'live and let live' attitude, expressed in a relaxed lifestyle. Both peoples value the good things in life, speak with similar accents and enjoy the same type of food. The only 'odd one out' in the convent appeared to be Mater Priscilla, a Westphalian, with all the characteristics attributed to North-Germans: sternness, discipline and a certain lack of tolerance and humour.

Teaching my sweet, polite and hard-working girls proved very satisfying. It also gave me a wonderful feeling of self-confidence and independence. True, I'd never wanted for anything while at school or at home due to a most generous father who'd have bought me the world, had I asked for it. But now, for the first time in my life, I could go out and get anything within my means without having to ask for it. My first salary was spent on a radio and other items to give my dark room a more personal touch: a few pictures and ornaments, a bright bedspread and table cloth and lots of books.

But my job in Wasserburg turned out to have one major draw-back. Living in, I had to abide by the same rules as the convent boarders and my social life was non-existent. Joining the local theatre club at least ensured monthly coach tours to Munich. I was amazed to see so much bomb damage in the Bavarian capital ten years after the war, but Munich's theatres and concert halls still flourished.

On 9 December, my twenty-first birthday, I was overwhelmed by all the attention, cards and presents I received. But Mater Priscilla's wish left me speechless.

Class III (Commercial College in Wasserburg/Inn, Bavaria) after their Finals (August 1957). I am in the centre of the first row.

'Congratulations, Fräulein Jutta, on your coming of age,' she smiled. 'Let me just say on this important occasion how well you fit into our community. Have you ever thought of joining the order? Please, give it some serious consideration.'

I couldn't believe what I was hearing. Becoming a nun was the very last of my intentions. To show that my interests in life stretched well beyond the convent gates I spontaneously booked a trip to Paris for half term. This didn't have the negative reaction I expected but my 'vocation' was never mentioned again.

Having completed my first year at Wasserburg I decided to take a different, more scenic route home. A leisurely boat trip on the Danube from Passau to Krems would be a splendid start to my summer holidays. Only one occurrence spoilt my enjoyment of the cruise: the stories of a group of East Germans about life in the DDR. Yet they weren't the only Europeans still suffering Soviet rule.

Back in West Germany in the autumn I heard the distressing news of the Hungarian revolt. Radio reports described the bloody battles between demonstrators and Russian tanks, and worried letters from my parents kept mentioning the massive floods of refugees into Austria.

Another tragedy was threatening world peace in 1956: the Anglo-French handling of the Suez crisis, regarded as aggression of Communist-backed Egypt, caused a split with America and world-wide moral outrage. Being a long way from home made me perhaps react more anxiously to the political turmoil of the time. But with no immediate job prospects in my homeland, to stay on in Germany was my only option.

That, nevertheless, my second Wasserburg year was most enjoyable I owed to the company of my fellow-Austrian, Marietta. Like me, she had been recommended for her first post by the sister-college in Krems. Marietta was a stunning young lady. Her slender build and pale complexion, contrasting with beautiful dark eyes and hair, gave her the appearance of a graceful Meissen figurine. Marietta was also a high-flier with two main ambitions in life: a distinguished academic career combined with the ideal marriage. My friend's vision of her future husband amused me. He had to be tall and good-looking, blond and blue-eyed, and well educated with a prominent position.

'She's certainly realised her ambitions,' I thought when, ten years later, the new Ph.D. introduced her husband to my family. Not only was Bernd blond, blue-eyed and handsome, he also had a top job as a leading civil engineer in Bavaria's road building programme. But, after our return visit to her luxurious home in Regensburg, there was an incredibly messy divorce. Poor Marietta! Her 'ideal marriage' had been very short-lived.

But back to 1956/57, the carefree year two young Austrian teachers spent in a Bavarian convent: Marietta and I shared many interests and enjoyed each other's company. I practically lived in my friend's room, which was at the front of the building and much larger and lighter than my own. It was Marietta's idea to start a 'Teach yourself Italian' course and to try our hands at dressmaking. Two dirndl dresses each were the proof that we'd been quite successful in the latter. Marietta was also enthusiastic about our monthly theatre trips to Munich but, like me, found the city's October Beer Festival overrated and lacking in entertainment.

Most weekends we explored the sights and scenery of rural Bavaria. 'Mad King' Ludwig's palace on Lake Chiemsee was only a short train ride from Wasserburg and so was Berchtesgaden, Hitler's former mountain retreat. We loved rowing on the nearby Königs-See surrounded by majestic snow-capped peaks. We visited famous tourist and winter sport centres like Oberammergau and Garmisch-Partenkirchen and spent many weekends at Kufstein or Kitzbühl, their charming Austrian counterparts. During the carnival of 1957 Marietta and I had the privilege of seeing the 'Schäffler-Tanz' performed in Wasserburg. Severe frost and snow and temperatures of -30°C could not stop this ancient custom which, like the Oberammergau passion plays, dates back to the times of the Great Plague.

'To defy the Black Death and cheer up their distressed fellow-citizens,' Mater Vincentia informed us, 'a few young "Schäfflers" (apprentice brewers) decided to perform their colourful dances in the deserted streets. From that day on the plague claimed no more victims and the grateful Wasserburg people vowed to repeat the "Schäffler" dance in their town every seven years.'

During the following spring both Marietta and I received visits from our parents. While Mama and Papa fully enjoyed their Bavarian weekend, Herr and Frau Schröder's memories were less happy. A letter to their daughter summed up their experiences:

'My dear Marietta,' it began, 'we were so pleased to see you and the beautiful town of Wasserburg. But our journey home seemed doomed. It was all because of the overhaul we had done on the car at that Wasserburg garage. Well, those repairs turned out to be anything but cheap. It is illegal to have your car done up in Germany if it isn't registered there, the customs officer informed us (the shiny new back wings gave the game away!), and charged us DM300.00. As we hadn't enough money on us to pay the extra fine we had to leave the beetle behind at the border and travel home by train. God knows when we'll get it back. You can imagine how your dad misses the car in his job . . .' It took almost two months of wrangling and waiting before the Schröders' VW was released.

At the end of the summer term Marietta decided to stay on in Wasserburg for another year before resuming her studies at Regensburg University but I thought it better to leave for home. By now my name would be top of the waiting-list and I dare not risk missing a job at an Austrian school. My hopes were dashed. The education authority stated with regret that the Zwettl district, responsible for my employment, still had no immediate vacancies in the area's primary schools.

Trying to soften this blow, Omi came up with a brilliant idea.

'You heard me mention my relatives in Meran, haven't you, Jutta?' she said. 'I'd like to visit them before my eyes become too bad to travel. You know Opa and his reluctance of going abroad. Perhaps you could come with me?'

Our Italian holiday turned out marvellous for both of us. While Omi was Aunt Dina's guest on the outskirts of Meran, I stayed with her other niece, Lilli, 'Under the Arches' in Old Town. Aunt Lilli, a war widow, had three children around my age, two of them still living at home. They were all bilingual and a charming mixture of Austrian and Italian temperaments. I instantly made friends with Anneliese, the youngest daughter, who introduced me to all her pals. And when her brother, Richard, was not climbing mountains he loved to take me out on his treasured Lambretta. My parents would have died had they seen me riding side-saddle through the mad Italian traffic. But all local youngsters were so lively, so carefree and not at all safety-conscious and it was easy to get carried away by the southern spirit. The day when we finally had to say, 'Arrivederci, Merano!' came far too soon for Omi and me.

RASTENBERG

Arriving home after my 'Italian adventure' I found a wonderful surprise waiting for me. 'Could you spare me a minute, Fräulein Jutta?' Pfarrer Wiesinger, our new parish priest, approached me after Sunday mass. 'Count Thurn is looking for a private tutor for Marina. Would you be interested in the post?'

Of course, I was! This job offer couldn't have come at a better time.

As Lord of the Manor and patron of Rastenfeld church, Count Thurn of Rastenberg kept a high profile in our village. Almost two-metres tall and rather aloof, he had the air of the typical Austrian aristocrat. In contrast, his wife, petite, dark and lively, could not deny her Latin origin. I'd heard of the tragedy when a mystery illness claimed the Thurns' second son, Johannes. Their remaining children were teenagers Georg ('Giorgio') and Christoph, ten-year-old Marina and Baby Raymondo. While his boys attended exclusive boarding schools it was the count's wish that his only daughter should complete her first high school year privately at home. I seemed to fit the bill as her tutor and my interview was a mere formality.

Arriving at Rastenberg castle at ten one morning, I was ushered into an elegant room and invited for coffee with her ladyship.

'Marina will be here shortly,' the countess assured me, and carried on chatting about anything and everything under the sun. Half an hour passed before my prospective pupil appeared. Marina was tall for her age and wore a wry smile, tousled dark hair and trousers which looked like her brother's hand-me-downs.

'Say hello to Fräulein Schweighofer! She'll be your teacher for the next year,' said the countess. Marina attempted a curtsy, and a grubby little hand was placed into mine. Visibly relieved that the introduction was over, she dashed back to her play-mates, passing her father on his way up. The references supplied by the head of a German girls' college seemed to impress his lordship. Conditions of employment were discussed and, within minutes, the new private tutor to the count's daughter left Rastenberg castle.

Following the strict syllabus laid down by the education authorities I soon discovered the reason for my appointment. Without individual

Rastenberg Castle – high above the Purzelkamp Valley where I taught Marina von Thurn, in 1958.

tuition Marina stood little chance of being accepted at high school. Her vivid imagination helped her to write splendid essays but her spelling and numerical skills left much to be desired. A general lack of concentration did not help matters and required much patience. The only subject Marina really excelled at was P.E. To raise my charge's educational standards seemed a tall order but hard work and mutual fondness did eventually bring success.

Marina fascinated me. Not at all what one expects from a young lady of the aristocracy, she liked nothing better than playing boys' games with the sons of the count's employees.

'I hate it when we have guests and Mami makes me wear a dress,' she once confided in me. Poor Marina! There were always visitors at the castle, where writers, painters and composers kept rubbing shoulders with members of the aristocracy. I recall one incident when coming face to face with one of the count's distinguished guests caused me some embarrassment. Marina's lofty room, overlooking the castle rock's drop to the Purzelkamp valley, was our classroom for most lessons, but for music we used the drawing room. I was just trying to pick out a tune on the grand piano when the door opened and a stranger appeared.

'I am so sorry! I do apologise,' he muttered and left immediately. I had forgotten about the gentleman until, two hours later, we met again. It had been snowing heavily all morning and the countess insisted I'd stay for lunch before walking home. It was all very grand, with a butler in white gloves serving at the table. But I nearly choked on my steak when being introduced to the guest who'd overheard me teaching music. It was the well-known composer, Gottfried von Einem, whose opera *Danton's Death* I had heard – and utterly disliked – in Munich only months before.

The Foresters' Ball, a big event in Mariazell's carnival calendar, was a good excuse to visit Uncle Joschi and family again. My recent experiences at Rastenberg castle had my uncle roaring with laughter. A former employee of the present count's father, he too, had some good stories to tell. Reminiscing over life in Rastenfeld my uncle and aunt enquired about old friends like the Brandtners and Österreichers and, most of all, Mama and Papa.

'You will tell them to come and see us soon, won't you?' they insisted. 'Of course, thank you,' I said, 'but I doubt my parents will take up the invitation. They get busier and busier and never seem to have time for holidays.'

Uncle Joschi and Aunt Milli would have been amazed to see the advance in our business. When restarting in 1947 Papa had decided against replacing the machinery lost to the war effort. Home-produced building blocks, roof tiles and pipes were far too labour-intensive to be profitable these days. Instead, my dad had his materials delivered from factories, wholesalers and quarries. When the outbuildings and the newly concreted yard proved insufficient for storage it was time to expand. A large hangar on land next to Opa's orchard now served as the Schweighofer's main depot.

To ensure efficient deliveries Papa then had invested in his own transport. He'd bought an estate-car and a truck-cum-trailer and employed a full-time driver. Inevitably, the rapidly growing concern had brought more work for my parents. While Papa kept busy drawing plans, working out estimates and inspecting the sites, Mama's domain was stock control, wages and the rest of the office work.

The mounting workload had made Papa quite dependent on the help of a young colleague. Peter, the son of a builder they'd known for years, would have made the ideal son-in-law for my parents. A pity, that my own feelings towards unobtrusive, hard-working Peter never exceeded those for a family friend. The more everyone sang the praises of Papa's splendid assistant, the more paranoid I became about him. Hearing his car pull up at the front, I would immediately disappear through the back, into my room or upstairs.

'What on earth do you dislike about Peter?' Mama kept saying. 'You don't even know him. Why not give him a chance?'

Papa said nothing but clearly disapproved of my 'inexplicable behaviour'. How could I get through to my parents that I wasn't really a bluestocking, uninterested in men or marriage, that I longed to meet 'Mr. Right' but I knew in my heart Peter wasn't 'it' and that, watching the business take over their lives, I could never marry a country builder?

It was no good. Mama kept on expressing her worries over my 'attitude towards men' and the dangers of falling for the wrong type. My mother's lack of understanding distressed me. Lucky her to find the partner for life at a very young age! That I hadn't found mine I blamed on spending ten years of my youth in convents and another two living at home.

Only Omi seemed to understand my dilemma.

'Be patient, my love, and don't get upset,' she would reassure me. 'When the time's right you'll find the right man.'

At the end of term my mind was made up. Come what may, I would not spend another year living at home. With Marina passing for class two of a private high school in Vienna, my mission at Rastenberg was completed. Surely, after four years of waiting, that job at an Austrian state school had to materialise soon.

KIRCHBACH

Did the Zwettl education authorities get tired of my enquiries or had my name at last reached the top of the waiting-list? About this I could only surmise, but in June 1958 the miracle happened: I was offered a job at an Austrian state primary school.

The letter was brief and to the point:

'Dear Candidate,

I have the pleasure to inform you of your appointment as a probationary teacher at the county primary school of Kirchbach, Zwettl county council. Would you please sign and return the enclosed contract to this office and report to the head teacher, H. Bernecker, as soon as possible.

N. N.

The Education Authority's Office

Zwettl, Lower Austria.'

This wonderful news took some digesting, and tiny shadows of doubt kept dampening my ecstasy: how would I cope with infants at a village school after three years of teaching at college and grammar school level?

'It'll be a challenge, but fun,' I convinced myself, scanning the map for an obscure place called Kirchbach. I finally located the tiny hamlet in the Upper Waldviertel, some 15 kilometres west of Zwettl. As defined by its name, Kirchbach's main features were the church and the stream. You couldn't miss the only other important buildings, the pub and the school.

Kirchbach Primary School, my first state school where I taught in 1959.

Small farmhouses and crofts, scattered among gigantic boulders, made up the rest of the village. The school was definitely Kirchbach's most modern structure. Built on a hillside, it enjoyed views over the village and beyond. Cream walls and a steep brown roof harmonised pleasantly with the soft green of the meadows and the white stems of the silver birches. The school's interior was practical and cosy: a spacious hallway with miles of coat- and shoe-racks led to centrally-heated, airy classrooms with picture windows, beech furniture and floors, and dark green blackboards. You could hardly see the classroom walls for posters and children's art work.

The headmaster, Herr Bernecker, was a charming man with wavy silvery hair, a kind, craggy face full of laughter lines and a preference for corduroy jackets and breeches.

'Welcome to our school, Fräulein,' he said, seizing my hand with a tight grip. 'I hope you'll be happy in Kirchbach.'

'In there you'll find your little lot, the six-to-eight-year-olds,' he explained, pointing to one of the classrooms. 'I take the older ones in class two. Any questions or problems, and you know where to find me.'

'I'll show you round while it's quiet,' he said, collecting the keys from his office. 'I hope you have time to come home with me later. My wife is longing to meet you.'

Frau Bernecker, small, round and chirpy, was waiting for us in the doorway.

'I'm so pleased to meet you, Fräuleinchen (little Miss). Please, come in and have tea with us. Hans, will you bring a chair for our guest?'

I warmed immediately to the wife of my boss, known in the village as 'Kirchbach's First Lady'. ('She even has the nerve to tell Herr Pfarrer when it's time for a hair cut!' I later heard my landlady snigger.)

I was made so welcome in Frau Direktor's hospitable home that most of my free time was spent there. We exchanged books and knitting patterns, pored over fashion magazines and generally enjoyed girls' talk. Herr Direktor was just as sociable; more a father figure than a superior to me. He found me a room in a house near the school ('Frau Wagner is a bit bossy, but a good sort and fastidiously clean'), recommended the village pub for its cooking ('After a morning at school you'll be ready for a good meal. One does get hungry when teaching') and, most importantly, showed me the ropes of the job I'd come to do. With Herr Bernecker's help I soon learned to deal with three different age groups in one class and how to draw up the 'Jahresplan' (plan for a whole term's tuition) and 'Wochenplan' (layout for every lesson a week ahead). Checked and signed by the Headmaster, they had to be shown to the school inspector should he call. I loved my little country-bred girls and boys, especially the 'babies' who still needed help with blowing noses and buttoning coats and forever got their wellingtons mixed up.

As a village like Kirchbach had little to offer outside school hours, my weekends were spent at home or in Zwettl and my holidays further afield.

'Some of us have relatives in all the best places,' the Berneckers joked as I returned from a winter break in Zell am See with Willi and family. And Frau Direktor was really envious of my invitation to a grand Viennese ball. The surprise letter had come from cousin Lotte, who in 1945 had shared the ordeal of the Russian raid on our house. Expecting her first baby, she did not fancy accompanying her doctor husband to the annual medics' ball. Would I like to stand in for her as Gerald's partner? she asked. Naturally, I accepted. The splendour of the Hofburg in the heart of Vienna was perfect for such an exclusive event. The State Opera Ballet, gracefully interpreting waltzes by Strauss, performed the grand opening, and dance bands were playing in most rooms of the palace throughout the night. A strict dress code demanded tails for men and long ball gowns and half-masks for ladies.

'What a fabulous outfit! You look stunning, Jutta.' Gerald's compliment on my gold, fur-trimmed dress was flattering but I was disappointed at his reluctance to dance.

Sponsoring my cousin Silvia at her confirmation in Linz – spring 1959.

'A ball like this is to see and be seen, not to dance,' my partner explained.

'It's far too crowded for dancing, anyway,' I consoled myself and heaved a sigh of relief when at midnight the masks were allowed to come off. Mine had been such a nuisance forever steaming up my glasses underneath.

'Give me provincial balls any time where everybody knows everybody and you hardly miss a dance,' were my real thoughts when thanking Gerald and Lieselotte for this unique experience.

On Whit Sunday Uncle Willi's daughter was to celebrate her confirmation and I had been asked to act as her sponsor.

'Oh, Jutta, what a great idea!' Silvie had shrieked when I suggested Linz cathedral as the best venue.

On the day my young cousin looked just beautiful, dressed all in white. The ceremony over and the traditional photo-session behind us, we sat off on a pleasure boat down the Danube. Silvia's parents met us in Krems and drove us to Friedersbach for a grand family gathering.

'What a shame, it's back to school in the morning!' was my little cousin's only regret. Her sentiment was shared by her teacher father and her sponsor.

Spring 1959 brought another joyful event, the fifth anniversary of our Matura and a reunion in Krems. How wonderful to see the familiar faces again and to hear what had happened to all my friends since we parted.

'Hello, I'm so pleased to see you! You haven't changed a bit!' was the general comment between laughs, hugs and handshakes. Everyone seemed to be present, former class mates and teachers, and there was great excitement as stories were told and photographs passed around. Helga, now teaching at a Zwettl primary school, was the first to be married. Her husband, 14 years her senior, had been a class mate of my Uncle Willi. There were ah's and oh's when the new Mrs. Zöhrer showed pictures of Hermann, their baby daughter, and their lovely house on Zwettl's outskirts. Loisi, the organiser of the reunion, had only recently returned from Hamburg. She was engaged to Fritz Staudinger, a law and economics graduate, and hoped to settle in Vienna. Irmi, her fellow au pair in England, was back in Austria, too. Encouraged by her former employer, Jo Grimond, she now studied modern languages in Vienna, aiming for a career with Austrian Airlines. Inge's 'tales of woe about a poor Tyrolean mountain school teacher' had everyone roaring with laughter.

'But there's a happy end to the story,' she chuckled. 'Cinderella did find her prince. They will be wed soon, live in the "kingdom of Weyer", Upper Austria, and intend to have lots of children.'

We all knew about Inge's resolve to marry only a tall man in order to produce 'normal sized' offspring. Apparently, it had been love at first sight when, one Christmas, she met this handsome big soldier travelling home on the same train and, as Inge concluded, 'things have developed from there'.

Not everyone's story had ended happily. Waltraud was one of only three not to attend the reunion. An unmarried mother, she was too embarrassed to meet up with her former school friends and teachers. Working as a nanny for a rich family in Turin, she had lost her job – and her Italian boyfriend – when she became pregnant. Poor Waltraud! Life was to bring more tragedies for the girl who'd always been so sweet and naive.

Soon after the reunion I received a surprise letter from the Education Authority in Zwettl.

'Dear Frau Kollegin Schweighofer,' it read. 'You have been selected for a transfer to Gross Gerungs primary school beginning with the autumn term of 1959. Please contact the headmaster, F. Bruckner, as soon as possible.'

'I shouldn't really say that, as Gross Gerungs means promotion for you,' was Herr Bernecker's reaction to my news, 'but I'm extremely sorry to lose you.'

As for me, I was devastated. I hadn't realised that placing teachers in Austrian schools was such an autocratic process, that all vacancies were filled from the top and probationary teachers and their headmasters had so little say in the matter. Being at the very bottom of my career ladder, I couldn't refuse an offer that would move me up a rung. But, after only one short, happy year in Kirchbach it was hard to say goodbye to my boss, his good lady and my dear little pupils.

GROSS GERUNGS

The person most excited about my new posting was Frau Brandtner from the grocer's shop.

'Have you heard? Jutta is going to teach in Gross Gerungs,' she told all her customers. 'That's my home town, you know, a lovely place with a great school; I'm sure she'll like it there.'

To a point Frau Brandtner was right. One of the Waldviertel's larger settlements situated some 20 kilometres south-west from Zwettl, Gross Gerungs was a vibrant market town in most pleasant countryside. Compared with the one in Kirchbach, my new school seemed enormous, providing both primary and secondary education under one roof.

'I assure you the premises are nowhere large enough to accommodate all our pupils,' Direktor Bruckner, the head of both sections, was quick to point out. 'Therefore some of the juniors have to be taught in the afternoons. I'm afraid your class, Two A, will be one of those affected, Frau Kollegin.' There was an air of authority about my new boss, a man in his fifties, of immaculate appearance and a precise, military gait and voice. As headmaster and Burgermeister, Director Bruckner held the most prominent position in Gross Gerungs. By word and example he kept impressing on his colleagues the crucial role they had to play in the community, both in and outside school. In practice this meant we had to be available not only for extra-curricular activities like sports, plays and outings, but also on bank holidays to supervise our pupils during festivities organised by council or

Gross Gerungs School – where I taught in 1960/61.

church. In addition, I frequently 'had the honour' of dealing with some of my boss's extensive paperwork.

Teaching a class of well-motivated seven-year-olds, all on one level, was child's play. But to maintain the excellent reputation his school had with the education authority, Director Bruckner kept a strict eye on his teachers at all times. Used to the headmaster sitting in on our lessons, we felt less nervous when the school inspector, Helga's father, came – always unannounced – to check on probationary teachers.

Director Bruckner's scrupulous regime was probably the reason for Gross Gerungs' outstanding results at the 'Befähigungs-Prüfung', the exam which followed two years of probation and secured permanent status to primary school teachers. However, it wasn't all hard work at Gross Gerungs. The happy atmosphere of the staff-room, where most personnel were in their twenties and unattached, well compensated for the head's strict formality.

For the first time in my life I had the chance to mix with single, like-minded men of my own age both professionally and socially. Being in the same situation broke down the barriers and made colleagues into friends. In groups of six to eight we would meet at pubs and cafés and enjoy films,

The Corpus Christi Day procession in Gross Gerungs (1960).

Gross Gerungs: fancy dress party in my class.

dances and outings. We felt at ease with one another and had lots of fun.

Then Alexander entered my life. A tall young man with a sparkling personality, he had left his private teaching post in Vienna to return to his native Waldviertel. Alexander's volubility and ready wit was unmatched by anyone I'd met before. He also turned out to be a high-flier and an excellent dancer, two more qualities I admired in a man. Did Papa ever guess why his daughter suddenly turned down his lifts back to Gross Gerungs in favour of two tedious bus rides? But how could he imagine my joy and anticipation of seeing a certain young man board the bus and, smilingly, head straight for the seat next to mine . . . the warmth and excitement when our bodies touched and his hands enclosed mine? There was no denying: I was deeply in love with Alexander. The attraction seemed mutual. Finding the height of fulfilment in each other's company, Alexander and I distanced ourselves from the rest of the colleagues and became an almost inseparable pair. The euphoria lasted five months. Then, all of a sudden, Alexander's behaviour changed. He appeared strangely quiet and distant and even seemed to avoid me. In the end I could stand it no longer and asked for an explanation. My hope that I'd imagined it all was dashed by a series of blows, delivered sentence by sentence:

'I've been thinking of the future and the career I hope to carve out for myself . . . There is no room for a serious commitment yet . . . It wouldn't be fair to expose a girl like you to gossip . . . People do jump to the wrong conclusions, so we shouldn't be seen in public together . . . But, of course, we can still remain friends . . .'

Oh, Alexander! I would have gladly waited for him until he'd realised his career ambitions. But, obviously, his priorities were different from mine and so were his feelings. I was devastated. My love had been rejected and my pride seriously hurt. Perhaps Mama was right in her assumption that I tended to fall for the wrong type of man. One thing was clear; I couldn't comply with Alexander's suggestion to be 'just good friends'. For weeks I felt faint and unable to concentrate on my work when Alexander merely entered the staff-room.

To come to terms with my disappointment I channelled all my energies into work and studies. My exam results with distinction had given me permanent status in primary schools. Now was the time to aim for higher qualifications. Holding a teaching certificate in shorthand since 1955, I needed to pass exams in two more subjects to make up a group. My choices were English and German.

A recent break in Malta had revealed that, after six years of neglect, I'd forgotten much of my favourite language. The result: an even greater drive to resume my studies in English so that I could teach it one day. Secondary school courses were held every Tuesday, and interested teachers could apply to have their lessons arranged over the other working days. So, from September 1960, four colleagues from the Gross Gerungs area, myself included, would travel 140 kilometres every week to attend the courses in Krems. While German, with its stress on medieval idioms proved rather boring, the English course was simply brilliant. What pleasant surprise to find Professor Mittermeyer, my heart-throb at college, as my tutor once again.

It was during that autumn that I received a most distressing telephone message: Papa had been rushed into hospital in Zwettl; could I come and visit as soon as possible? The news came as a great shock. Apart from the odd rheumatic attack, shrugged off as a legacy of the war, my father, to my knowledge, had never been ill before. What a relief when the acute gastric complaint turned out less serious than first feared. After ten days in hospital Papa was allowed home, but had to keep to a strict diet and avoid stress and exertion. Due to a gum infection my dad also had to have his teeth extracted. Regarding them as his most attractive feature, I was far more upset about that than Papa himself. His illness had made my father realise how much he'd allowed work to rule his life.

'When was the last time we've walked in the woods together?' he asked Mama from his hospital bed, adding the promise: 'It's high time we went on that holiday in the sun you always talk about . . .' But, of course, it was never realised.

Peter had managed to keep the business going in Papa's absence and it was not long before my workaholic father was living on site again.

Omi's health, too, gave us cause for concern. Blind in her right eye, she lived in constant fear that her troublesome left eye would also give up and throw her into complete darkness. Her mind as alert as ever, poor Omi found it extremely frustrating that she could no longer read, write or sew, let alone enjoy the wonders of television recently introduced to our home.

Abandoned were the visits to the spa town of Hall and even the daily walks round the village, so much enjoyed by my grandparents, stopped. While Opa still pottered about in the orchard Omi had no desire to leave the house or even her seat by the radio. She'd become very frail but would always buck up at the weekends when I was due home.

'Have you heard the news about Seibersdorf, Jutta?' Omi asked me one September day in 1960. 'Isn't that Dr. Staudinger married to one of your school friends?' She was quite right. The man who had spearheaded Austria's first nuclear power-station and hoped to take charge of the whole enterprise, was indeed Loisi's husband. However, the grand opening never happened. The people of a country so rich in hydro-electric power, were totally opposed to the new atomic reactor and its position close to the capital city. Mothballed after a referendum, Seibersdorf became a museum and a bit of a joke. They said Dr. Standinger never got over the disappointment of seeing his life's work in ruins. One Christmas Eve, years later, he was found hanging from the rafters of his exclusive country house.

ZWETTL

In early 1961 I received the offer of a transfer to Zwettl. Honoured that, only six months into my course, I should be trusted with teaching secondary school pupils, I gladly accepted. Life at Gross Gerungs had never been the same since my split with Alexander and the time seemed right for a change of scenery and a new challenge.

Director Bruckner was anything but pleased over my promotion. 'Why is it that Zwettl always robs me of my best teachers?' he ranted. Upset more than flattered, I found my boss's remark rather tactless, especially as it was made in the staff-room with everyone present.

Zwettl – The main square with the column of the Holy Trinity.

Zwettl with the secondary school in the centre and the convent in the background.

My colleagues' reaction was totally different:

'Good for you, Jutta!', 'Well done!', 'Congratulations on this important step up!' . . . I was really touched by all the handshakes, hugs and pats on my back followed by a most generous send-off, and almost regretted having to leave Gross Gerungs by Easter.

Sophie Dirnberger, Aunt Poldi's sister, was quite enthusiastic over my transfer to Zwettl.

'You are most welcome to lodge with us, Jutta,' she said. 'Martha and Lisl are only home during holidays and the odd weekend. So, if you like, you can have their room during term.'

I was more than pleased with this arrangement. At the Dirnbergers' house I would be part of a happy, generous family. Their lovely daughters were now studying in Krems, but Franz junior, in his last year at high school, and young Wolfgang, would still be at home.

'You might have heard of our neighbours, the legendary Grössls,' Sophie said, pointing to the villa next door. 'They have five daughters, all teachers and well-known for their splendid work, especially with the youth of the parish. Traute, one of the twins, has lived in America for a while but came back when her father died. She now teaches in Zwettl and looks after her senile, frail mother. I'm sure you'll like Traute; I'll introduce you.'

Sophie was right. Being neighbours and teachers at the same school, as well as studying for our English qualifications, Traute and I soon became very close friends.

Providing secondary education for pupils of a wide catchment area, my new school was much larger than its Gross Gerungs equivalent. It offered three classes for every year: an A-stream for boys (AK), an A-stream for girls (AM) and a mixed B-stream. Only about 50% of the 20-odd staff were proper secondary school teachers. As one of the other half, still studying for full qualifications, I was once again under the head's close supervision. But what a difference between my previous and my present boss! Director Marosz was quiet, unassuming and very popular with pupils and staff.

'One of our English teachers, Frau Wittich, retired,' he said, 'and you, Frau Kollegin, have been recommended as her replacement. I hear you are attending the course for Secondary English, so you shouldn't have any problems in teaching the subject. But if you need help or advice, your counterpart, Kollege Weinberger, will gladly assist you.'

Egon Weinberger, the school inspector's son and my classmate Helga's brother, proved supportive and very friendly. Fully qualified, he was a very good teacher and, like Traute, had gained practical knowledge of the language in the US. While Egon was in charge of English for boys I'd teach the subject to the girls of the A-stream. Among my pupils were Ingrid Österreicher, my friend's daughter, and Poldi Schrammel, the future wife of my cousin. My own class, 1 AM, 33 lovely, bright ten-year-olds, I took also for German and music. Through teaching shorthand to all final year pupils I became also tutor to Wolfgang, the Dirnbergers' younger son, and my cousin Karl from Friedersbach.

There was a great atmosphere among the Zwettl staff, true professionalism combined with generosity and kind-hearted spirit. But, with an average age of 38, most colleagues were married, and eligible young teachers few and far between. I did like Andy Müller who was happy-go-lucky with a great sense of humour. Pity, he was already spoken for. Another participant in the secondary school course, Andy was only too pleased to act as unpaid chauffeur to his colleagues, so Traute and I were able to travel in style in his chic white Ford Anglia. Thanks to cheeky, extrovert Andy, our study trips to Krems were always fun. We'd visit pubs for meals and drinks and dance to the latest pop tunes on the Wurlizer organ.

We felt entitled to some light-heartedness and fun among new clouds of political turmoil. Once again war seemed imminent as East and West disagreed over a world-wide nuclear test ban and the crisis over Cuba. Glued to the television in the staff-room, we all followed the Kennedy-Krushchev meeting of June 1961 in Vienna ; regrettably, it ended in stalemate.

Even more worrying was a problem nearer home. The Communists had found the perfect solution for stopping the mass exodus of East Germans to the west. The 'Berlin Wall' caused outrage and condemnation, but nothing was done about the 'illegal restriction of movement' in that unfortunate city. As top politicians on both sides argued their cases, ordinary folk kept asking themselves: 'Will the Cold War ever end?'

A music lesson with my class (IAM) in Zwettl (1962).

TWENTY-TWO

THE ROOTS OF A DEMON

Not long after my transfer to Zwettl Inspector Weinberger, Helga and Egon's father, retired and a new school inspector took office. Most interested in the local history of his new administrative district, Dr. Trischler, a scholar and author himself, called upon local teachers to pool their individual knowledge in an anthology of the Waldviertel. For me, an article by high school teacher Dr. Merinsky about the connection of Hitler's ancestors with the army training ground of Döllersheim made fascinating reading.

Dr. Merinsky's research is based on Döllersheim's parish register which, surprisingly, was not destroyed with the village and church but taken to my own parish of Rastenfeld and kept there throughout the war. The author points to entries of the birth, marriage and death of a certain Maria Anna Schicklgruber whose infamous grandson was to provoke the most profound changes of the 20th century. A closer look into Maria Anna's family history revealed that, for many years, she was in service with a wealthy Jewish family in Graz called Frankenberger. Pregnant at the age of 42, she returned to her home village, Döllersheim, and in 1837 gave birth to a son. Entering the illegitimate birth of Alois Schicklgruber into the register, the parish priest left blank the space for the name of the child's father. The fact that for 14 years Maria Anna received a paternity allowance from her former employers led many to believe that Alois's father was a member of the Frankenberg family and therefore a Jew.

In 1842 Maria Anna married Johann Georg Hiedler, an unemployed travelling miller. Too poor to look after 5-year-old Alois, the couple put him into the care of his uncle, Johann Nepomuk Hiedler.

Despite the disadvantages of his birth and poor background Alois became a success. His guardian, proud of the fully qualified customs inspector, wanted to make his nephew's birth less of a mystery. In 1876, long after his brother's death, he persuaded the parish priest at Döllersheim to alter Alois's birth certificate, making it read that Georg Hiedler accepted paternity of the child. His new surname spelt incorrectly, Alois Schicklgruber, at the age of 39, became Alois Hitler.

I couldn't help thinking that history might have taken a totally different course had it not been for that fatal name change. Would the German nation ever have accepted a leader with a name like Schicklgruber? And what about the snappy Nazi salute? 'Heil Hiedler! ' or indeed 'Heil Schicklgruber!' would certainly have lacked appeal for the Germanic ear! Truly hooked on the great Fürher's obscure family background, I was determined to find out more. My later research revealed amazing facts, conveniently concealed from the nation while Hitler was in power: The residential customs official in the border town of Bramau/Inn for many years, Alois Hitler, was hardworking and conscientious. But he also had a record of being emotionally unstable, perhaps even mentally disturbed. And there is evidence that his flexible conscience often made him manipulate rules and records for his own ends while maintaining a facade of legitimacy. Stressing the plight of his two small motherless children by a previous marriage, Alois obtained papal approval to marry his niece, Klara Pölzl.

At 24 she was only half his age and pregnant by him while his wife was still alive. Having lost three children in close succession, Klara, on Easter Saturday, 20 April 1889, gave birth to a son, Adolf. The little boy became the apple of his mother's eye. Concentrating all her interest and affection on him, she pampered and admired and never scolded him. Could this attitude towards her only son have been the source of the enormous sense of importance, of having a mission to do anything he wanted, which is so characteristic of the tyrant Adolf Hitler? To the delight of his devout mother Adolf's beautiful voice gained him a place as a choir boy at the Benedictine monastery at Lambach. The most ardent wish of the young boy was to become a priest. Standing on a kitchen chair with an apron as a vestment, he would deliver long, fervent sermons to an imaginary congregation.

When Alois retired, his relationship with his son deteriorated. According to his sister Paula, the boy received daily thrashings from their father. Psychologists suggest that Hitler's family structure with the brutal, dominant father and the passive, subservient mother and children may have created the image of a totalitarian state within young Adolf's subconscious. The trauma of Hitler's family subsequently became the trauma of the German nation.

When in 1903 his father died, Adolf and his mother and sister moved to Linz, the provincial capital of Upper Austria. He began to lose interest in education at 'Realschule' and was allowed to leave in order to realise his ambition of becoming a great artist. An ardent admirer of Richard Wagner, Adolf loved opera and also showed talent for drawing and painting. At the age of 18 he went to Vienna to study at the Academy of Arts, but twice failed the entrance examination.

Pretending he was indeed a student at the academy he dreamed of 'redesigning Vienna' and writing an opera, Wieland the Smith, attempted but never completed by Richard Wagner.

But reality was quite different from Adolf Hitler's delusions of grandeur.

Refusing work on the grounds of being an artist, he became a down-and-out. He slept on park benches and relied on soup kitchens and other charitable institutions to survive. He teamed up with a tramp called Hanisch, who sold the picture postcards Hitler drew. While living in a hostel in a predominantly Jewish district of Vienna the self-pitying figure of the young Adolf Hitler was exposed to a new wave of anti-Semitism. The Jews, so often persecuted by both church and state, had once again become a convenient hate object for a dissatisfied people. Propaganda leaflets branding them as 'subhuman' and 'a threat to Aryan culture' convinced Adolf that only the Jews were to blame for the nation's troubles as well as his own destitute plight.

In 1913, to avoid conscription into the Austrian army, Hitler left Vienna for Munich. His life changed dramatically when a year later the assassination of Archduke Ferdinand of Austria signalled the beginning of World War One. Hitler promptly joined the Bavarian Infantry Regiment and in war found his true vocation. Admiring the discipline and courage of German soldiers, the Austrian soon became more German than the Germans. Enraged by the 'disgraceful' Treaty of Versailles at the end of the war, Hitler sought vengeance for the 'shocking injustices done to the Fatherland', vowing to 're-conquer the place among nations to which Germany was entitled'.

The period of political turmoil and economic disaster following the war resulted in Adolf Hitler's spectacular rise to power. After his visit to Germany, David Lloyd George, the former British prime minister, wrote this article, 'I Talked to Hitler', published in the Daily Express, 17 November 1936:

'I have now seen the famous German leader and also something of the great change he has effected. Whatever one may think of his methods – and they are certainly not those of a parliamentary party – there can be no doubt that he has achieved a marvellous transformation in the spirit of the people, in their attitude towards each other, and in their social and economic outlook . . . One man has accomplished this miracle. He is a born leader of men. A magnetic, dynamic personality with a single purpose, a resolute will, and a dauntless heart . . . As to his popularity, especially among the youth of Germany, there can be no doubt. The old trust in him; the young idolise him . . . It is the worship of a national hero who has saved his country from utter despondency and despair . . . He is the George Washington of Germany . . .'

There were also spectacular successes in foreign affairs. Within five years Hitler regained much of what had been lost to Germany by the Treaty of Versailles. But it took two decades before his great ambition, a united Austria and Germany, could be realised. 12 March 1938 finally brought the Anschluss. Hitler marched in triumph into the capital of his native country ,which, until then, had rejected him and his political dogma. I'd heard of the day Vienna welcomed the 'Führer' and his troops with delirious enthusiasm.

Much later I discovered that this impressive show of Austrian fervour had been helped along by an equally impressive show of German organisational power: Nazi supporters from as far as Czechoslovakia had been brought into Vienna to cheer and shout and salute the Fürher with 'Heil Hitler!'

Only weeks after the Anschluss the village of Döllersheim, birthplace of the Fürher's grandmother and father, was destroyed by the Wehrmacht and the surrounding area turned into the largest artillery range of the German Reich. At the same time the Gestapo received orders to search Vienna for the tramp Hanisch and have him killed. Historians cannot explain the logic of these actions. Could Adolf Hitler, the superhuman being in the eyes of so many, have employed such drastic measures to cover up his own dubious past?

My parents and grandparents in 1961.

TWENTY-THREE

THE ENGLISH EXPERIENCE

LONDON

'Do you really have to go abroad in such difficult times?' Mama fretted over my plans to attend a London language school in the summer of 1961.

'I'm afraid so,' I said, planting a quick kiss on her cheek. 'You know how important practical experience is for my English course. I can't possibly wait until the Russians stop arguing with the West over nuclear arms, Cuba and Berlin. Besides, Lucy Spacek, the colleague who wants to come with me, is only free during July/August. But don't worry, Mama, we'll be all right.'

I was glad I didn't have to travel to England on my own although Lucy wasn't really a close friend. I'd met the platinum blonde at the English course in Krems where she kept a high profile among the other teachers. There was something about her appearance and frivolous charm that made male colleagues swarm around Lucy like bees round a honey pot and, aware of her magnetism to the other sex, she liked to play one infatuated admirer against another. With no travelling experience abroad, Lucy had left all the arrangements and bookings to me. She seemed enthusiastic about my choice of course in London's West End and the 'typical English host family' selected by the language school. We also agreed on the train as the best means of transport for us.

Unlike my parents, Omi was thrilled about my forthcoming journey to England.

'How marvellous to see a country which still has a monarchy,' she mused. 'Just imagine all the pomp and pageantry! I wish I was coming with you. But as I can't I'd like you to do me a favour, Jutta. You know about my nephew, the one with the Jewish wife who emigrated when Hitler took over. I haven't seen Franz since 1938 but have kept his address. Here it is. He lives in this small English town whose name I can never pronounce. Do you think you could look him up for me?'

'I'd love to, Omi, but it won't be possible,' I said, having scanned the map for a place called Harrogate. 'You see, Uncle Franz lives in the north of England, much too far from London.' I promptly regretted my hasty reply as disappointment clouded my dear grandma's face.

'Never mind then, my love. It was just a thought. But do make the best of this great opportunity; enjoy London and see as much as you can.'

And enjoy England we did, although we found it quite different from the country portrayed in films, school books and holiday pamphlets. To start with, our hosts were anything but 'the typical English family' advertised in the brochure. Despite living in Britain for many years, Mr. Hutchin, a Pole, and his Spanish wife, Laura, still spoke English with the most prominent native accents. However, proud and defensive of their adopted country, they regarded themselves more British than the British. This attitude was a constant source of amusement for Lucy and me. We got to know our landlords as kind, generous people with a wealth of local knowledge who soon made us addicts of that peculiar, strong brew the English called tea.

The Hutchins worked hard to maintain their terraced north-west London home and provide their children, Tony, twelve, Andrew, eight, and six-year-old Tina with everything they possibly wanted. Mr. Hutchin thought it an honour to be employed at the prestigious Harrods Store, while Mrs. Hutchin, more practical and less proud than her husband, cheerfully supplemented his modest income by charring and letting rooms to foreign students and a lodger, Kenneth Mason . . . A single man in his early forties, he had spent most of his professional life in Kenya until a serious leg injury ended his career in the police force. Though forever maligned as 'utterly boring', his present desk job seemed to provide Ken with plenty of money for his main hobbies, a big car and regular nightly tipples at his local.

So that we'd be in good time for the selection test Ken offered to take us to school on the first day. The Kensington School of English was not exactly what I had expected of a 'reputable private summer school for foreign students'. But, despite its unconventional location at a pub off Kensington High Street, it proved to be just that. Lucy and I found ourselves in the top group tutored by a student of linguistics, Christopher Dowling. My fellow Austrian nearly choked with laughter when he introduced himself to the class.

'Would you believe it, we've got a teacher called "Darling",' she told the Hutchins and Ken. The name 'Darling' stuck, although his signature on our work sheets proved otherwise. Darling's lessons were interesting and varied. They ranged from exercises in advanced grammar to essays and discussions on the latest media reports. One topic, the prospect of Britain joining the Common Market, was also the cause of many heated discussions in the Hutchins' house.

With school ending at lunch time, the afternoons and weekends were ours to explore the city and see for real those unique institutions we knew only from text books. Though London's vast underground system proved most efficient for getting around, Lucy and I much preferred the unique red double-decker buses. We relished the splendour of Westminster Abbey and St. Paul's Cathedral, delighted in the pageantry of Buckingham Palace and the Tower of London, took advantage of the famous museums and art galleries (all free of charge) and the brilliant Oxford Street shopping and saw as many West End shows as we could afford. We found London simply amazing, unmatched by any other place in the world.

But it was the British people who really intrigued us.

'I wonder where all those typical starched Englishmen are hiding?' Lucy reflected. 'You know, the ones with bowler hats, umbrellas and the proverbial stiff upper lip. If you ask me, the Brits aren't as formal as the Austrians. Even the bus drivers here call you "love", "duck" or "darling"!' I agreed with Lucy. Coming from a country where titles were all important, and used to the address of 'Fräulein' plus surname, I found the familiarity of first name terms among strangers rather odd.

We considered the British incredibly honest and trusting. It was common practice to leave front doors open and cars unlocked in the streets. At newspaper stands you could help yourself and leave the money in an open container. Shoplifting, it seemed, was unknown in the London of the early 1960s and so were vandalism, graffiti and litter. Orderly queues at bus stops, check-outs and box offices testified to British patience and discipline, but what Lucy and I admired most in our host nation was their tolerance, fair play and respect for the individual, no matter, how cranky. Where else but in London could you voice your opinion on any subject from a soap box in a main centre park? Where else in the world would you see such a colourful mixture of races, cultures and creeds living together in a true cosmopolitan manner?

As well as gaining experience of the British and their capital city, my fellow Austrian and I also got to know each other better during this interlude. Lucy probably thought me an easy touch, naive enough to be manipulated, too reserved and conventional to pose a threat; all in all a useful travel companion. As for me, I kept cringing over Lucy's vanity and her tales of past conquests. And it was beyond me how any girl could seriously consider eloping to Israel with a young Jew she knew only as a spectator at Buckingham Palace.

But there were also compensations with a travel companion like Lucy. An admirer of hers, Ken would regularly meet us from school and drive us around London and even as far as Stratford-on-Avon. And, most importantly, without Lucy I would never have met Brian.

'I don't want to go home just yet,' she moaned near the end of our course. 'Wouldn't you like to stay in England for a little longer, Jutta?' 'Depends what you've got in mind,' was my cautious reply.

'Have you heard of Scarborough in Yorkshire? According to Kneale Marshall, the English pen friend of my student days, it's a seaside resort on the East coast. I've lost touch with Kneale but have hung on to his address.

Might get invited to Scarborough if I play my cards right. But you've got to come too, Jutta. I wouldn't dare go by myself.'

'My, what a crafty Clara you are,' I said reading the letter Lucy had written to Kneale's family. 'The bit about "your own and your friend's holiday of a life time", our "desire to see more of wonderful Britain" and our "deep regret over having to leave at the end of the course" really tears at your heart strings. If this cajolery doesn't lead to an invitation I'll eat my hat.'

'You might have to do just that,' warned Lucy as the days went by without a reply from the Marshalls.

At last the letter with the Scarborough postmark arrived. It was from Kneale's mother and read something like this:

'Dear Lucy, It was lovely to hear from you again. I'm sorry your letter took so long to reach us but we've moved house and now live in Hillcrest Avenue (see new address!). We'd be happy if you and your friend came to stay with us for a while when your course in London has finished. Unfortunately, Kneale is no longer at home; he's working in Canada as part of his post-graduate studies. Our daughter, Thelma, the dancer, is on tour in Germany at the moment but our elder son, Brian, will be delighted to look after two young Austrian ladies . . .'

'I knew it, I knew it, we'll be off to the seaside!' Lucy waved the letter containing this good news. She became even more ecstatic when our landlord described Scarborough as a top British holiday resort. The excitement was catching and I, too, began to look forward to our journey north.

SCARBOROUGH

Having reached York at 6 am after what seemed an endless journey through the night, I wished we had not taken the Hutchins' advice to travel by coach. Making the best of the two hours' wait for the Scarborough train we had breakfast and a quick wash at the nearby railway station, put our luggage in store and began to explore the city of York. A brisk walk along the medieval wall soon blew the cobwebs away and we could only stand and stare at the awe-inspiring Minster.

At Scarborough station we found Mrs. Marshall waiting for us. A warm, talkative lady, she greeted us like old friends.

'I'm sorry that Brian couldn't come to meet you by car,' she said insisting on helping with our heavy suitcases, 'but the shop is so busy with holidaymakers at the moment, Father just couldn't manage without him. So, I'm afraid you have to put up with little old me, and another tedious bus ride.'

Listening to the lady's friendly chatter we found the Yorkshire accent quite different from the Oxford English we had been taught. But we had no trouble in understanding our hostess, who kept complimenting us on our command of the language.

'Can't wait to see the sea,' announced Lucy, scrambling to the top of the double-decker bus which was to take us to Scarborough's outskirts.

'I'm sorry, dear, but service buses don't go anywhere near the front,' Mrs. Marshall explained, 'but our house is only a short walk from the North Bay.'

It was a most pleasant route along the parks and gardens of residential Newby, dominated by those famous English lawns and hedges and an abundance of roses everywhere.

'Brick buildings seem to be most popular here,' I observed, 'and they're not plastered like ours at home but have brightly painted doors, eaves and fall pipes.' A builder's daughter, I was intrigued by the architecture of different countries. The term 'semi-detached' was another novelty for me. Mrs. Marshall described this style as two houses under one roof but Lucy wouldn't have it. All she could see, she insisted, were two flats, side by side in one house.

The Marshalls' home in Hillcrest Avenue was what she called 'a proper' house (detached), a most attractive, ivy-clad stone building surrounded by colourful, well tended gardens.

Mrs. Marshall led us straight up to the first floor.

'This is where you sleep, my dears,' she said, opening the door to a bright, cosy bedroom. 'It's normally Brian's, but he has to make do with the room in the attic when we have guests. How d'you like the view over North Cliff golf course? Handy for a golf addict like my son, isn't it? Can just slip through the hedge when he feels like playing a few holes after work. But I am talking too much. You poor girls must be exhausted. Make yourselves comfortable and have a little rest. I'll see you downstairs when you're ready to eat.'

That was Yorkshire hospitality at its best. Chatting about our first favourable impressions of Scarborough we unpacked and freshened up a little. Then, the sleepless night finally catching up with us, we flopped on our beds and, within minutes, were fast asleep. Emerging again half-way through the afternoon, we found a refreshing salad meal waiting for us in Mrs. Marshall's sparkling kitchen. We felt at home.

At six o'clock the men arrived from work. Mr. Marshall, thin with a prominent nose and a stern expression, seemed quite the opposite of his extrovert, warm-hearted wife. But Lucy and I agreed there was only one word to describe Brian: dishy. Slim with brown hair and even features, he was very good looking and had the most beautiful hands I'd ever seen in a man. Quiet and unassuming, he had a delightful sense of humour and an innocent boyish charm, quite unusual for a man of 27.

Lucy and I were introduced to the most popular meal of the region: fresh fish straight from the sea, followed by trifle, another delicacy of British cuisine. After dinner, clearly following his daily routine, Mr. Marshall settled down in his armchair with a cigarette and the evening paper while Brian changed into casual clothes to take his guests on a tour of the town. His pride and joy, the turquoise-and-cream little sports car, was already parked on the drive. It was really a two-seater but neither Lucy nor I minded having to squeeze up to Brian. We soon saw that Scarborough deserved its name of Britain's most scenic seaside resort. It had a unique coastline of two moon-shaped bays, divided by a steep, rocky headland on which stood the remains of an enormous castle.

'This is the Spa.' Brian pointed out an ornate domed building on the South Bay. 'In Victorian times members of high society flocked here to "take the waters". That was Scarborough's heyday when it was known as "The Queen of Watering Places".

These days our town attracts quite a different type of holidaymaker, more what we call the "bucket-and-spade brigade". The Spa is now used for conferences, dances, shows and concerts.'

'That's where I spent most of my youth.' Driving along Valley Bridge Brian pointed to the old Boys' High School. 'And this is what followed on.' We'd stopped in the town centre at a small Tudor-style building which, in gold lettering, bore the sign 'J. B. Marshall & Son, Family Jewellers since 1936'.

Our host had left the highlight of the evening for last. 'International motor-bike races are run here twice a year,' he explained, while carefully negotiating the numerous sharp hairpin bends up Oliver's Mount.

But Lucy and I were more interested in what we'd been promised as the final surprise. We were not disappointed. The view from the war memorial at the top was breathtaking. At our feet lay a jewel of a town. The brick-red of its buildings surrounded by green parkland contrasted pleasantly with the gold of the beaches and the sapphire blue of the sea. We watched the sun set in a blaze of fire and, within minutes, Scarborough had adopted an even more romantic aura. Suddenly, illuminations appeared everywhere: floodlights emphasising the town's historic sights, white lights resembling strings of pearls competing with their reflections in the sea, and multicoloured fairy-lights transforming tree-walks and gardens into a children's wonderland. Our eyes wandered from the picturesque little harbour along the distinctive silhouettes of the castle, the ancient parish church of St. Mary's and the Grand Hotel and back to the Victorian elegance of the Spa.

We were enchanted with Scarborough.

The next morning, armed with maps and guide-books, Lucy and I set out to learn more about this beautiful town. We discovered that Sir George Cayley, the Father of Aeronautics, and the actor Charles Laughton were born here, that the literary Sitwell family had their home in Scarborough and that Anne Brontë was buried in the churchyard of St. Mary's. Naturally, we sampled all the delights a typical seaside resort provides. Aboard the pleasure boat *Coronia* we'd admire the changing views of Scarborough's superb coastline, weld sail on the *Hispaniola* to Treasure Island to 'make our fortune', we'd take long walks along the cliff tops and colourful gardens and, most of all, we'd enjoy the sea bathing and lazing on the beach.

But the highlight of our day only came when Brian arrived from work and took us on yet another scenic drive through the beautiful countryside around Scarborough. My favourite route led through the rugged North Yorks Moors so radiant in their summer dress of purple and pink heather. Who could resist the charm of Robin Hood's Bay, once a notorious smugglers' post, now a haven for writers and artists? Who could be indifferent to the historic port of Whitby, the home of Captain James Cook and Caedmon, the Father of English Sacred Song? Viewing Whitby's attractions from the height of St. Hilda's Abbey was not enough for Lucy and me. We'd insist on descending the 200 steps to the Old Town and climbing up to the West Cliff on the other side. We'd take each other's photos under the archway of giant jaw bones, the unique reminder of Whitby's whaling industry of the past and, gazing at Captain Cook's monument, we'd marvel over the achievements of the town's most celebrated son. Looking out to sea, the explorer's eyes seemed fixed on the spot where the spooky Count Dracula had come ashore.

In our eyes Whitby was an incomparable place with lots to offer to locals and visitors, young and old.

The route inland in a westerly direction became another favourite of ours. It led through pretty villages, each with a charm and history of its own. Ayton, nearest to Scarborough, with an extensive building programme under way, didn't impress me too much at the time. Who would have thought it possible that, within three short years, I would call it my home?

Lucy and I just loved picturesque Brompton, which held many childhood memories for Brian and was the birthplace of his sister, Thelma. Everything here seemed to recall the aviator pioneer Sir George Cayley and the poet Wordsworth, who made his marriage vows in the old village church. A spot very popular with tourists was scenic Thornton-le-Dale boasting a little stream, a well-known, well photographed thatched cottage and numerous souvenir and craft shops. You needed more time than an evening to explore the old market towns of Pickering and Helmsley, each crowned by a majestic castle; trips to such distant havens were usually reserved for weekends. Lucy and I both fell in love with charming Hutton-le-Hole on the fringe of the North Yorks Moors, a place as quaint as its name, while the magnificent ruined abbey of Riveaulx left us breathless. Built by Cistercian monks, it showed a surprisingly similar layout to its Austrian counterpart, Stift Zwettl. Another lasting experience was the stroll along the sheer drop of Sutton Bank. Torn between the sweeping panorama below and the gliders' silent elegance above, we could hardly keep our eyes on the path leading to the amazing White Horse of Sutton-under-Whitestone Cliffe. Descending the steep incline to the valley, the path finally led to Ampleforth College, a renowned boarding school for Catholic boys.

On numerous occasions Lucy and I had admired Brian's driving skills; we also knew him as a motor-sport enthusiast. A trip to Flamborough Head, south-east of Scarborough, revealed his other great passion, golf.

'It was my pal, John Allison, who introduced me to the game,' Brian told us. 'We met in the Air Force in Cyprus doing National Service. We've been members of Flamborough Golf Club for a few years now and play there most Sundays. I'm sure, you'll like Flamborough and my mate, John.'

And so we did. A bank clerk from the neighbouring resort of Bridlington, John Allison was a pleasant young man, well educated, entertaining and funny. He explained the history of the old lighthouse which, unfortunately, was closed for visitors that evening. But a stroll along Flamborough's bizarre chalk cliffs, reflecting the colours of the setting sun, more than compensated for that disappointment. The path along the cliff top led past Flamborough's exposed golf course but, aware of our ignorance of the game, the boys kept golf talk to a polite minimum.

Later that week we met two more friends of Brian's, Walter and Peter.

'I've known those two since we were lads, building and flying model aircraft together,' he said, introducing them.

Walter, a jovial moustachioed man, a good deal older than Brian, presented us each with a beautiful rose from his garden, which promptly earned him the name 'The Cavalier of Roses.' As much as I liked all his friends, none of them, in my opinion, could hold a candle to Brian. Not surprisingly, Lucy thought the same. She began to apply all her charm, in the attempt to win his favour.

'What am I doing wrong, Jutta? It's not fair but he's got eyes only for you,' she kept complaining.

'Don't be silly,' I said. 'You're imagining things. Brian is lovely to both of us and treats us exactly the same.'

But in the end Lucy's remarks made me think. Was there a man who might prefer my reserve to the frivolity of the almighty charmer? But what if he did? I was 26 and far too sensible to expect a short holiday romance to develop into something more serious. Determined not to get hurt again, I dare not admit to myself, let alone to Brian, how much this young Englishman meant to me. It wasn't until our last day in Scarborough that I realised the attraction was mutual.

We'd been to the Black-and-White Minstrel Show at the Futurist Theatre and later for a walk in Peasholm Park. What happened after this romantic night out was not the usual friendly goodnight kiss. This kiss was quite different, so different, it made me tremble . . . Tomorrow we'd be leaving for home but I was looking forward to seeing Brian again on his return visit to Austria.

Listening to my glowing account of London and especially Scarborough, my family probably guessed it wasn't the sights and scenery that formed the strongest attraction. But only Omi got to know more about a certain young Englishman called Brian Marshall. However, one aspect of Scarborough was never mentioned between us, its closeness to her nephew's present abode. The meeting, so important to Omi, could have been arranged easily had I only taken his address with me. 'But I hadn't, so, to avoid further disappointment, I kept quiet about Harrogate and Franz Maier.

Not long after my visit to England I lost my beloved grandma. Delayed by a school exhibition I had arrived home later than usual that Saturday, only to find Omi had died two hours before.

'She's kept asking for you, Jutta,' a tearful Mama received me, 'but we saw no need to alarm you . . . She'd been ill for only three days . . . We had no idea that it was the end . . .'

I was devastated with grief. If only I'd been with darling Omi before she fell asleep . . . to hold her skinny little hand and tell her how much I loved her . . . Now she had left us forever . . . There was no comfort in thinking that Omi had reached a good age (84), that she had been spared complete blindness, and her death was sudden and painless. I began to dread the weekends at home where everything reminded of Omi. It took months before I could cope with the loss of the person who'd been so much a part of my life. It was during that difficult period that Traute Grössl proved a true friend. Urged to drop in next door for a coffee and chat whenever I wanted, I always found sympathy, understanding and reassurance from Traute. Most evenings we would spend studying English together, which proved a great help for both of us.

There was no sign of Lucy when the course in Krems started again in the autumn. Had she lost interest in her studies, we wondered. The bombshell dropped when, weeks later, she suddenly reappeared.

'I found more amusing things to do on my day off with my English guest,' she was quick to tell everybody.

'What d'you mean? Brian hasn't been in Austria already?' I asked dumbly.

'Oh I'm sorry! of course, you don't know,' Lucy seemed slightly embarrassed.

'He arrived at the end of September. Took my advice not to travel by car. Let him use mine for getting around. Had a wonderful fortnight together, even managed a trip to Vienna. But there wasn't really enough time to fit in a meeting with you.'

I was speechless with fury and disappointment. So Lucy did get her man in the end. How could Brian ignore and shun me like this? But then, had I ever encouraged him in the slightest, shown my attraction for him? Too late now. My stupid reserve had ruined my chances with a wonderful guy. Who could blame Brian for choosing the more gregarious girl? The blame was entirely mine for trusting a woman like Lucy.

'May I ask what all that was about between you and our mutual friend?

You looked daggers, Jutta!' my colleague Andy enquired on the way home.

'Lucy and I happen to disagree over someone from England, if you really must know,' I retorted. And Andy had enough sense not to pry any further.

Dear Mrs. Marshall had not forgotten my birthday. She loved writing letters and kept me informed about all the family news.

'I've been cross with Brian for not visiting you in Austria,' she said, and after that tactfully avoided the issue. The greatest forthcoming event at the Marshalls' house, I heard, was daughter Thelma's February wedding to a Berliner called Hans-Georg Raabe. But it was Lucy who crowed about another forthcoming visit of Brian's. I did not give her the satisfaction of seeing me hurt or even surprised, nor did I invite them to Zwettl.

'By the way, I'm going to England again in the summer,' I announced. 'I really look forward to seeing the beautiful south coast.'

There was no further mention of Brian's Easter visit or the holiday job Lucy was seeking in Scarborough. Having at last completed my project on T. S. Eliot's dramatic works, I was ready for my summer break in Bournemouth.

BOURNEMOUTH

Arriving at the elite south coast resort one July day in 1962, I realised why my landlady found it necessary to let rooms to foreign student. Her house on the outskirts of Bournemouth was in poor repair, the carpets were worn and there were holes in my bedspread. Mrs. Brown, an elderly widow, lived alone with her pampered Labrador dog, Sandy, and received only rare visits from her pub landlord son and the granddaughters she adored. A simple, kind soul with a passion for cooking, Mrs. Brown went into great trouble to produce the very best of English cuisine for her guest, herself and, of course, Sandy.

Unlike my previous language school, the Bournemouth School of English was run from a proper college building, vacant during the summer holidays, and located among the parks and gardens of an elegant residential suburb. My class tutor, another language undergraduate, taught strictly from the book. Media reports on everyday events had no room in Nigel Sanderson's lessons.

Although it catered for as many foreign students as the Kensington School of Languages, there were fewer groups at the Bournemouth school.

Each combined different levels, mine consisting of mainly French and Belgian high school pupils. They'd come to England in organised parties and preferred to keep themselves to themselves. Having different priorities and interests, the only three mature students, Kirstin from Hamburg, Luigi from Milan and I, soon formed a little group of our own. School outings and study trips along the south coast provided ample opportunity to get to know the area and one's fellow students. Kirstin and I hit it off right from the start. An attractive, vivacious young lady, she loved showing photographs of her beautiful home on the Alster, her parents and boyfriend Jan, and expanding on how the Bournemouth summer school would benefit her business studies course at home. Kirstin felt very strongly about Germany's east-west divide and the Berlin crisis. On the first anniversary of the 'wall of shame' I found her upset and anxious.

'What's happening in my country, Jutta?' she lamented, pointing to a newspaper report in front of her. 'Imagine, there is this 18-year-old East Berlin boy climbing the wall to escape to the West. Machine-gunned in the back by his own people, he bleeds to death while the murderous guards look on. There is nothing the West German police can do except throw him bandages as he lies there screaming for help . . . The outraged West Berliners who gather in protest against the wall and its latest victim are also attacked by old "Goatbeard's" henchmen. And this is the state of Germany seventeen years after the war!'

If Kirstin was an open book, Luigi was not. I sometimes wondered why the high-powered executive had chosen an exclusive British seaside resort, not for a holiday, but to brush up his rusty school English amongst a gaggle of foreign teenagers. Luigi Rossi, a charming, sophisticated man in his middle thirties, was never very forthcoming about his home and family circumstances. His Latin temperament made him quite partial to the ladies – I saw him cry when Marilyn Monroe's suicide was announced – and there was no wedding ring or any other indication of a possible Signora Rossi. One day on a cruise around Poole Harbour a newspaper article caught my eye: 'Oscar-winning actress Sophia Loren had to cancel plans to make a film in London. After six years of marriage the Italian film star and her divorced husband, the producer Carlo Ponti, are to face bigamy charges in Rome . . . '

'What do you make of this?' I said, holding the newspaper under the nose of my chain-smoking Italian friend. Luigi's face changed colour as he read the report.

'In my country divorce is – what is the word? – illegal; you did not know, Jutta? Italian law says I'm married man although Carla divorced me five years ago. No woman, no love life for me in Italy . . . not easy to live like monk. I'm broken man, Jutta, believe me, finito, kaputt . . .'

With his secret out in the open, Luigi's behaviour towards me suddenly changed. Misunderstanding my compassion for his dilemma he seemed no longer satisfied with being just friends. I had to stop his advances.

'I'm sorry, Luigi," I spluttered, 'the only reason for my being here is to better my English. I don't want to get involved, not with you or anyone else.'

But was that really the truth? My thoughts kept returning to another English holiday romance which, sadly, came to nothing. Yet it, seemed wrong to tell my Italian admirer he could never measure up to Brian. My bias extended much further.

In my opinion, the fashionable south coast with elegant Bournemouth, genteel Poole, magnificent Salisbury and the famous New Forest wasn't a patch on the scenic North East, with romantic Scarborough, historic Whitby, quaint Robin Hood's Bay and the rugged North Yorkshire Moors. However, the postcard with Tess of the D'Urbervilles' farm sent to my English tutor in Krems stressed my enthusiasm for rural Dorset. I sincerely hoped Professor Mittermeyer would take the hint and question me on Thomas Hardy.

My class teacher had very kindly checked over my thesis on T. S. Eliot, my weeks in Bournmouth had come to an end and I was ready to leave Britain for home. However, with the English exam due in October there was no time to relax. But all the hard work paid off in the end. Both Traute and I passed, despite not getting one single question on Thomas Hardy.

Lucy Spacek never entered the English examination that autumn. She had other, quite different priorities, we heard.

'I'm getting married in a fortnight,' she informed her open-mouthed colleagues, 'and about time, don't you think? Can't stay a spinster forever!'

Her intended was a young teacher from her school and new to the area. 'Poor Brian!' was my first response to Lucy's bolt from the blue, then, on reflection: 'Lucky for Brian.'

TWENTY-FOUR

FOR THE LOVE OF BRIAN

The letter arriving in early 1963 did not bear the familiar handwriting of Mrs. Marshall. It was from her son.

I opened the envelope with trembling fingers. My heartbeat increased as I read:

> Dear Jutta,
> This is a letter of apology. Disappointed by one young Austrian lady I now realise how stupid I was neglecting the other one. You must have been hurt by my ill manners not to contact you on my visits to Austria. Can you forgive me?
> I would dearly like to make up for my bad behaviour and come to see you, perhaps at Easter, providing, of course, your invitation still stands.
> Please, let me know soon.
Much love from
Brian XX

It was with very mixed feelings that I read and re-read Brian's letter. The guy I'd put on a pedestal had let me down. Why should I repeat my invitation he chose to ignore in favour of another woman? I had my pride and didn't like being second best. On the other hand, Brian had also been hurt and seemed disillusioned.

I had to show him that not all Austrian girls were alike. This was my chance to repay the Marshalls' hospitality. Yes, I owed it to Brian to be his hostess, but certainly nothing more . . . Immediately I started planning the most enjoyable holiday I could devise for my English guest. He might have to spend a few days in Zwettl until I broke up from school. I'd book him into the Hotel Loidl, owned by the wife of a colleague and most popular among local teachers. And I'd ask my Uncle Willi to accommodate us over Easter. Brian would like the grand mountain scenery around Zell am See and Salzburg.

With Zwettl hardly noted for foreign tourists, my prospective visitor from England soon became the talk of the town. Naturally, 'Jutta's English friend' was also the top of staff-room gossip.

'Fancy this bloke driving 1,000 kilometres to Austria at this time of the year! Can't be the weather he's bothered about. Something, or rather someone else, must be the attraction . . .'

I ignored my colleagues' teasing remarks but when the day came I could no longer contain my excitement.

'Hello, why is this exotic foreign car stopping at our humble work place? Any idea, Jutta?' Andy suddenly yelled, dragging me to the window. I blushed. Surely, it couldn't be Brian as early as this. But it was! He'd driven the 700 miles between Scarborough and Zwettl in one go! My pulse started racing as I dashed downstairs to greet him.

'How lovely to see you, Brian! Welcome to Zwettl!' I panted, quite embarrassed by his spontaneous embrace. 'You must be worn out after that marathon journey. Let me show you to your hotel. You'll need a rest.'

Aware of the grinning faces at the staff-room window, I quickly jumped into the smart little car. There were plenty more surprised glances as we made our way to the Loidl's hotel. It was from the Grössls' house that, after only an hour, I spotted a turquoise-and-cream car slowly coming up our hill.

'Here I am, Brian!' I shouted dashing out into the street.

'There was a certain ring in your voice, Jutta,' Traute told me later, 'that couldn't deny your real feelings for your English guest.'

At the end of the week, after a short stop at Rastenfeld, we were on our way to Uncle Willi's. Was I glad to escape my parents' probing eyes and the uneasy atmosphere at home!

'I'm only returning the hospitality I received from the Marshalls by showing Brian a bit of my country,' I said, defending my action of 'going off with this Englishman'. My parents didn't approve but could do little about it as I was 28-years-old.

On the long journey to Zell am See Brian talked a lot about Lucy.

'During my last visit her attitude towards me had changed,' he confessed. 'In the end I was only the chauffeur for her and her group of friends. I left for home quite disillusioned and haven't heard from her since.'

'That's unforgivable, Brian,' I sympathised. 'You must be terribly hurt. Let's try and forget about Lucy. One can only wonder how she'll shape up as a wife.'

Brian didn't know that Lucy was married.

'The poor bloke, I feel sorry for him,' he commented and managed a grin.

Once he'd got Lucy off his chest Brian began to relax.

'Please, let's not spoil this holiday,' I said, 'by mentioning her name ever again.'

My uncle and aunt took to their British guest right away. They both had a smattering of English and, with their daughter as chief interpreter, conversation was easy. Silvie, used to her grammar school English, kept giggling over Brian's Yorkshire pronunciation but he got his own back by constantly teasing my little cousin.

Following a very severe winter, spring had not yet reached Zell am See. The lake was still frozen and Austria's most famous mountain road, rising 8,000 feet to the Gross Glockner, was still inaccessible. But I was determined to show my English guest as much as possible of my homeland and had worked out a daily agenda. A visit to Salzburg was imperative and the road through the sheltered Salzach valley presented no problems for Brian's high-powered car. Yet we did get stuck the following day on Pass Thurn en route to Kufstein and Kitzbühl. On Good Friday we climbed the treacherous footpath to the waterfalls of Krimml. What did it matter that the world-famous cascades were still in their winter metamorphosis of icicle giants? We were holding hands and the severe cold couldn't prevent our hearts warming to each other. The Englishman and his Austrian hostess found themselves irresistibly falling in love.

I shall never forget the Easter Monday of 1963. Waking up to brilliant sunshine, my relatives had suggested a group outing to the Schmittenhöhe, a mountain that could almost be touched from their windows.

As soon as the cable-car had released its load of sun worshippers and skiers, Silvie was off down the piste to pursue her favourite sport. But Brian and I, donning very bright sweaters, were cajoled into becoming film stars for the day. It was fun, though slightly embarrassing, to act under my uncle's direction: 'Will you walk towards me holding hands! . . . Closer, much closer, please! . . . Now look at each other! . . . Smile! . . .'

But we did draw the line at kissing on camera. That was reserved for a more intimate hour later that day . . .

'Let's round off the evening with a walk by the lake. I mean just the two of us,' Brian said softly.

It was rather late when, starry-eyed, we returned to the warmth of the Schweighofers' living room. Willi and Ida exchanged meaningful glances.

Enjoying yourselves, are you?' smiled my aunt. Then, turning to her husband and daughter, 'Come on, dears, it's time we retired. Some of us have to be at work in the morning.' Another encouraging wink towards Brian and the door closed behind them.

It was then that I heard what I'd been longing to hear.

'Thank you for a marvellous time, Jutta,' Brian said, after a passionate kiss. 'You've shown me so much of your wonderful country and, what's more important, I've got to know you. I love you, Jutta, and want to be with you for the rest of my life. Could you, I mean, do you love me enough to leave all this behind and come to England with me as my wife?'

'I love you, too, Brian,' I declared without hesitation, 'enough to follow you to the end of the world.'

Several heavenly days succeeded that Easter Monday. Then, suddenly, we came down to earth with a bump.

Not used to ice-covered mountain roads, the British sports car gave up the ghost. It happened the day before our planned departure when all garages were closed for the weekend. Panic struck. What were we going to do? It was back to school for me on the Monday. I would have to leave Brian behind!

'Don't worry, Jutta,' said my unflappable uncle. 'You can travel to Zwettl by train. I promise we'll look after your Brian until he is leaving for home. I'm sure, his car will be fixed long before then.'

Deploring the breakdown, which robbed us of several more precious days together, we said our tearful goodbyes. It was a miserable journey for me alone on the train. A few more sleepless nights followed until I knew that Brian had safely reached English shores.

A greater dilemma loomed at the weekend: how to break my big news to my parents. Mama might understand, but not Papa with his choleric temperament and his prejudice against anything foreign. If only Omi had still been with us. She would know how best to solve this dilemma. But once Mama had got over the shock of my revelation I found I could talk to her woman to woman.

'I can see how you fell for a nice boy like Brian,' she said, 'but, Jutta, he's a foreigner and bound to be different. Ask yourself, have you really known him long enough to consider marriage? And, Jutta, do think very carefully about living abroad. England is a long way from home, should there be any problems . . .'

'Mama, I do understand your worries,' I said hugging my mother, 'but you needn't fret, I assure you. There is no doubt in my mind that Brian is the right man for me. I love him and want to be with him wherever he is. And, believe me, Mama, the English are no different from us, and the Marshall family's lovely. They've made me so welcome the first time around. Soon I shall know them even better. Brian has asked me to spend my summer holidays in Scarborough. Eight weeks of "intensive training" should get me used to their way of life. Everything will be O.K., so please, don't be upset.'

My mother seemed calmer after our little talk but still concerned about Papa's reaction.

'He'll be incensed and distressed, Jutta,' she said. 'Please, don't mention anything for the time being. We have to pick the moment very carefully to tell Papa about you and Brian.'

The right opportunity came sooner than expected. Rushed into hospital with acute appendicitis I was operated on the same night. Despite her anxiety about me Mama cleverly used the situation.

'As expected, your father took your news badly, she confessed at the first hospital visit, 'but don't worry, dear, he's much too concerned about you to upset you in your sick-bed. By the time you leave hospital he'll have simmered down and come to terms with the situation.'

Poor Papa! The last months had been quite traumatic for him. He had lost both his parents in close succession: Grandmother had died after a serious illness, Grandfather suddenly in his sleep. Then our driver had killed poor old deaf Tasso by reversing the lorry over him in the yard. And, to crown it all, Papa would soon lose his only child, to an Englishman of all people. Never mind brother Willi singing this Englishman's praises! How would he feel if his daughter married abroad? The dreaded showdown never happened but Papa's behaviour began to give us concern.

'He's walking about like a bear with a sore head,' Mama complained. 'If only held talk about his worries and get them out of his system.'

It was May, my favourite month, when I was released from hospital, but in view of the tense situation at home I opted for recuperation in Zwettl. Taking the best of the glorious sunshine I would sit in the Dirnbergers' garden relaxing, daydreaming and thinking of Brian. I would read his weekly love-letters until I knew them by heart and reply with long, passionate ones of my own. With pen and paint brush I'd recapture the wonders of spring, showing Brian how much everything around me reminded me of him.

The 'Bleeding Hearts' became tokens of our undying love, the fresh may green a symbol of hope, and the flowering cherry tree a giant bridal bouquet. These heavenly days ended all too soon when my return to school called for a more sober view of life. Thank God, the summer holidays were approaching fast and with them my reunion with my beloved.

Getting off the train at York station I ran straight into Brian's wide open arms.

'How sweet of you to collect me in York, darling,' I cried. 'I never thought you could get away from the shop.'

'Try and stop me, sweetheart!' His embrace was warm and intense. 'Couldn't be without you for another hour! Father can manage on his own for once. But, tell me, my love, what have you got in there? A ton of Austrian rock?' Carrying my suitcase, the other arm round my shoulder, Brian led me to the familiar turquoise-and-cream little car.

'Can't wait to see my parents' faces when I introduce their future daughter-in-law.'

'You mean you still haven't picked up the courage to tell them?'

'I just wanted you with me when I announce our great news,' he beamed.

'I know Mother will be over the moon. She really loves you to bits, Jutta. I'm not so sure about Father's reaction. Can be quite awkward when it suits him, you know.'

'Oh dear! Men seem to be all alike when it comes to their children's partners,' I sighed, describing my own father's conduct.

'Poor darling! What a bad tine you must have had. I only hope I can make it up to you and your parents.'

In contrast to Papa's, Mr. Marshall's response to our announcement was calm and unemotional.

'Will you stay in England or live in Austria after the wedding?' he asked his son. Several more questions followed:

'So you'll carry on in the business if I increase your wages and perhaps make you a partner? . . . How soon are you thinking of getting married? . . . Where will you live? . . .'

Satisfied with the answers, he added: 'We'll have to talk more about the financial arrangements when the time comes.' With that he picked up his cigarette case and the evening paper and disappeared into the living room.

Mrs. Marshall's reaction was totally different.

'Can't tell you how thrilled I am, Jutta!' she smiled hugging me tightly. How lovely to gain another daughter! Wait till I tell Thelma!

Brian had mentioned before that his sister, German brother-in-law and baby niece now lived in Scarborough. Brother Kneale, however, had decided against returning to England; he was completing his studies at the University of California at Berkeley, San Francisco.

Over morning coffee and afternoon tea (it's the other way round in Austria) I met and was warmly received by Mrs. Marshall's numerous friends. Mr. Marshall also became quite amiable, even telling me incomprehensible jokes. But, as I wrote to my parents, the sun for me only rose in the evenings when Brian came home from the shop. How I longed to be with him all hours of the day, but that was just wishful thinking. Work always had to come first, that seemed to be no different in England. At least, the Marshalls were able to close the door on their business and did not take it home with them, like my parents. And Mrs. Marshall, not directly involved, always had time for her family. A splendid cook, she fostered my interest in English cuisine by letting me copy and try her well approved recipes.

Step by step she eased me into the way of life which was to become my own pretty soon. And from day to day my relationship with my future mother-in-law became warmer and closer. My letters home were one buoyant account of my darling Brian, his lovely warm-hearted mother, Yorkshire hospitality and the generosity of the British.

'You won't believe this,' I remember writing, 'but not once have I felt a stranger in England. Everyone is so kind and supportive and makes me feel welcome and at home. Dear Mama, Papa and Opa, I'm so happy. I couldn't marry into a better family than the Marshalls.'

Planning our future together, Brian and I agreed on an early wedding. Both mature people, we hadn't taken this decision lightly. What was the point of a drawn-out long-distance courtship and an unnecessary delay of events? We decided on a formal engagement during Brian's autumn visit, a spell of house-hunting in Scarborough at Christmas and a spring wedding.

Returning home after two months in England I couldn't get over the change in Papa's behaviour. Was it the weeks he had time to think, my exuberant description of life in Scarborough or perhaps my radiant face that had softened his outlook? Whatever it was, I now found him open to rational discussion and more ready to listen. I explained how little difference there was between our two nations, that prejudice against foreigners no longer existed among the widely travelled younger generation and that my case was by no means unique. Had not several of our young relatives decided on living abroad?

Her marriage to a Viennese had not prevented Friedl Trappl from following her brother and emigrating to Canada. Martha Dirnberger, married to a Dane, now lived in Copenhagen while her sister Lisl hadn't thought twice about joining her Yugoslav boyfriend in a Communist country until he had finished his studies. If they all coped, so would I, being that little bit older. Distance was of no essence either, I assured Mama and Papa. Brian and I planned an Austrian holiday at least once a year and they would always be welcome in England.

'That's more than Uncle Joschi sees of his daughter, who only lives on the other side of Austria,' I insisted. 'Or would you rather have me at home as an unmarried mother like Ulli Brandtner?' They admitted they wouldn't. But one promise I had to take to my parents: to keep my Austrian citizenship, just in case . . .

'Cor! what a machine! Is it Bulgarian?' 'Don't be daft! GB stands for Great Britain. They've nothing like this in Bulgaria!' was the argument between two small boys drooling over the foreign car parked by the school.

During the last week in September Brian's smart vehicle had caused quite a stir among Zwettl's schoolboys. My girls, not surprisingly, showed much greater interest in its driver and owner. They soon figured out that the good looking Englishman who sometimes joined in their lessons was a very close friend of their teacher's. Like me they'd secretly watch for the distinct two-coloured car approaching the school around midday. They would then hang around to see 'Miss' join her English boyfriend in that 'fab vehicle' and drive off towards Rastenfeld. It was all very titillating and thrilling. Of course, there were more whispers and heads together and even greater excitement when finally a diamond ring appeared on teacher's finger.

We had done our best to make our engagement a memorable occasion not just for us, but also for Mama and Papa. In well rehearsed immaculate German Brian had formally asked for my hand in marriage, presenting his future mother-in-law with a bouquet of flowers. Permission granted, he then had slipped the three-stone diamond ring onto my finger. A toast to the engaged couple followed. It was all very emotional with hugs and kisses and, of course, some inevitable tears. I was so proud of my Brian. Against all the odds he had won even my father's approval.

The half-term holidays gave me the chance to show my fiancé yet another part of my beautiful homeland. Luckily, as Frau Direktor Bernecker once said, I had friends and relatives in all the best places. Vienna, the capital city and my place of birth, was the first stop on our East Austrian tour.

My class (IIIAM) in Zwettl (1963).

Inviting us to their town centre flat, the Trappls had made us extremely welcome. It amused me how well Brian got on with Uncle Silvester, who spoke not a word of English. Resorting to ingenious sign language, the two men never stopped laughing. Having seen most of Vienna's attractions, we moved on to Uncle Joschi's Styrian abode. Recently widowed and alone in his big house after Heidi's marriage, he too seemed to relish our company. An expert in local history, he was eager to show us yet another corner of beautiful Austria.

I was back in Zwettl after Brian's departure when a great tragedy sent shock waves all over the world.

'They have assassinated President Kennedy!' an upset Sophie Dirnberger called up to my room. 'I've just heard it on the seven o'clock news.'

I was stunned. The whole of Europe had been moved by the US President's recent West Berlin visit. With his famous statement: 'Ich bin ein Berliner!' he had identified with the town's citizens as representatives of the free Western world. Now the vibrant young leader, the victor in Cuba's raw power politics, had found an untimely violent death, and mankind was in mourning. Would the Kennedy policy of East-West reconciliation continue and finally secure world peace?

It was during this new political turmoil that I set out on another journey to England. But, despite the general unease, I was in high spirits. Brian and I were to face a most thrilling challenge, the purchase of our first house. To achieve this within my Christmas holidays seemed a tall order, so, to save time, I travelled by air.

Unfamiliar with the British property market I'd left dealings with estate agents, mortgage brokers and solicitors in Brian's capable hands. But I really looked forward to helping to choose our first marital home. What a relief to find all the spade work completed. Brian had compiled a list of all houses our savings plus Papa's substantial donation could buy. The selection process could start immediately, but still seemed to go on forever.

'I'd rather buy new as we do at home,' I confessed to my long-suffering fiancé, and I'd like a "proper" house, not one of these unfamiliar semis.' Dismissing the mostly old buildings on sale in Scarborough, we began our search in the villages. We both loved genteel Scalby but found its property prices well beyond our reach.

'There's a whole new estate going up in Ayton. Why don't you try there?' Brian's father suggested. And that's how we discovered our dream house, a three-bedroomed detached dormer bungalow in the eastern part of the village. On first sight it looked not far off completion and the builder proposed to have it ready for Easter. We believed him, put down the deposit and signed the contract. Our main mission accomplished, we had to decide on heating, general colour scheme and fittings for kitchen and bathroom. Then we searched Scarborough's stores for a suitable bedroom suite, our wedding present from Brian's parents. In the end we were totally exhausted but jubilant nonetheless. In just ten hectic days we had reached our goal. Mother and Father Marshall were dragged out in a blizzard to admire our lovely new house. Picking their way through the slush, mud and builders' rubble of our future front garden, they fully approved of 17 Chantry Road.

Back in Zwettl for my last term at school, I never stopped talking about my brilliant new home. Papa's doubts about its timely completion were dismissed out of hand. The builder seemed such a trustworthy person. Why should he go back on his word?

The tower of the church, Stift Zwettl, where we got married in 1964.

TWENTY-FIVE

YOU, HAPPY AUSTRIA, MARRY!

Maundy Thursday, 26 March 1964.

Bleary-eyed I squinted at my watch as the early morning train rattled towards Vienna. 6.30 am. Another hour before we'd reach Franz Josef Station, another hour and a half before offices would open . . . My mood was one of grim determination. If this mission wasn't successful my wedding would be in jeopardy! To think that, until recently, everything had gone so well . . .

Respecting our choice of venue, Pfarrer Wiesinger, parish priest in Rastenfeld, had agreed to marry us in Stift Zwettl and to make the necessary arrangements with the clergy and the boys' choir of the collegiate church. The civil ceremony which, under Austrian law, had to precede the church wedding, was booked at the register office in Zwettl for the same day.

Having decided on a honeymoon in North Italy, Brian and I had contacted my cousin Anneliese, an employee of Meran's tourist office, to make hotel reservations for us in early April. By Christmas I had handed in my notice at school, we'd bought a house, chosen the rings – at Marshalls' Jewellers, of course – and sent out the invitations. To let Aunt Poldi and Uncle Karl enjoy the day without obligation the reception was booked at the Hotel Loidl in Zwettl. However, most of our guests would be accommodated in Friedersbach, a most generous wedding gift of my uncle and aunt.

I had cajoled my fellow English teacher Egon into translating the sermon and other important features of the marriage service and there were to be English as well as German hymns. Uncle Willi had volunteered to record the entire ceremony on film while Photo Lux would take the traditional photos. I had tried on my dress, ordered the flowers, made the seating plan for the reception and chosen the menu. I was well organised and well on target. It was then that things began to go wrong.

From Brian's letters it had became clear that our house would not be ready for Easter. Bad weather conditions were blamed by the builder for the delay. Brian's parents had offered us accommodation as long as required but, naturally, we would have preferred to start married life in our own home. As it turned out that was not to be until the end of the summer.

We knew that Brian's brother could not be at the wedding and understood that his sister and brother-in-law hesitated to travel the long distance with a young child, but Mr. Marshall's sudden decision not to attend for business reasons came as a bit of a shock. The number of English guests was now down to four: Brian's mother, her close friends, Mr. and Mrs. Tinnion, and John Allison, the best man.

It may have been Mr. Marshall's example or last minutes' nerves that then made my father turn awkward. He bluntly refused to partner Brian's mother at the wedding as he wouldn't be able to converse with her. I tried to reason with Papa but couldn't make him change his mind.

'Just let him be, Jutta,' Mama tried to soothe my fraying nerves. 'You know your dad; he'll come round in the end.'

Dear Mama had just overcome a mini-crisis herself. She felt cheated of the pleasure of providing the customary dowry for her only daughter.

'Why do they do everything different over there?' she'd lamented, as I pointed out the contrasts in English and Austrian tableware and bedding. Grudgingly accepting the impracticality of transporting bulky electrical goods, heavy pots and pans and fragile crockery over thousands of kilometres, she had persuaded Papa and Opa to give us their value in money. But there was one item I simply couldn't resist buying: the delicate bone china dinner set I'd seen in a Krems' shop window still graces our table on special occasions.

The publication of the bans in early March had made me so happy. What a thrill to see my name linked with that of the man who would be my husband in a month's time! Then I suddenly realised that the Stift Zwettl boys' choir would not be back from their Easter break to sing at our wedding.

'No problem, Jutta. Leave the music to me,' my friend Traute assured me. 'I'll sort out something appropriate with your girls.'

There had been laughter and tears at the farewell party organised for me by staff and pupils. What a send-off and what lovely presents: the Book of Austrian Cuisine full of mouth-watering recipes and glossy illustrations, the set of delicately etched wine, beer and liqueur glasses, the leather-bound guest book with the drawing of Stift Zwettl church and the signatures of thirty girls . . .

Then, suddenly, the Easter holidays were upon us. On a last routine visit to the registrar I made an alarming discovery: the marriage licence had not yet arrived from the Vienna head office. And that less than a week before the big day! I began to panic. The missing document would not only jeopardise the civil ceremony, but also the church wedding, the reception, the honeymoon . . .

No more post could be expected after Good Friday and all offices would be closed over Easter. I couldn't wait any longer, had to chase up that vital document myself. So here I was en route to Vienna, my nerves on edge and my stomach churning.

Trying to trace one citizen's personal file in a huge government office block can be a harrowing experience. Sent from one room to another I still wasn't getting anywhere. Forced to describe my problem for the sixth time I finally broke down with frustration. At last a sympathetic official took pity on me and helped me hunt down my file. He took ages checking through it.

'It seems the department has not yet received your fiancé's tax declaration,' he observed. 'The charges for the marriage licence are calculated from that; therefore the delay.'

'I knew nothing about this English tax form, only that by now it was unobtainable as Brian would already have left for Austria.

'In that case,' concluded my friendly official, 'your only option for acquiring the licence is to pay the highest possible fee.'

Naturally, I hadn't got that sum of money on me but vowed to raise it, come what may. Back at the government office within the hour, I handed over Ö.S.2000,00 borrowed from Uncle Trappl's bank account. The precious document safely in my possession, I hurried home. The licence was in the registrar's hands just in time before his office closed for Easter.

I was triumphant. I'd beaten the red tape and saved my wedding. Time to relax now, to look forward to Brian's arrival.

Good Friday. The hours passed and the weather worsened. Darkness fell and still no sign of the English car with the groom and the Best Man. Around midnight I lay down on the living-room couch, but couldn't get to sleep for worry. It was 4 am when at last a car pulled up in front of our house. With joy and relief I sank into the arms of my beloved Brian and his mate, John. They both looked exhausted but wouldn't retire for a while yet. Over numerous cups of cocoa I heard of their horrific journey, the blizzards, freezing fog and accidents on the way.

'It wasn't until midnight that we reached Munich, the worst traffic nightmare I've ever known,' Brian recalled. 'I'd been at the wheel since nine in the morning, was dog-tired and got utterly lost. I had to let John take over and he drove the rest of the way. Managed Father's big car brilliantly although he'd only ever driven a Mini.'

John got his well-deserved pat on the back. Then it was my turn to describe my ordeal with the wedding licence.

'Am I really worth all that money?' Brian grinned.

'Every penny of it,' I insisted, finally kissing him goodnight at five in the morning. By lunchtime the pair had sufficiently recovered to face another 50 kilometres' drive to St. Pölten to meet Brian's mum and friends off the train. Mission accomplished, the whole English contingent then moved to Friedersbach where Willi and family had just arrived. With cousins Silvie and Karl translating, the language barrier soon disappeared. A few drinks at the pre-wedding party on Easter Sunday, and we were all one big, happy family; especially best man John and bridesmaid Silvie had become friendlier by the minute. Even Papa submitted to Mrs. Marshall's charm and declared himself honoured to be her partner.

Filming at a wedding was something unheard of in the Austria of 1964. But, as a former Stift Zwettl choir boy, Uncle Willi had obtained the abbot's permission. All Easter Monday he and Karl junior were up and down ladders like monkeys, rigging up lights all over the church and taking shots of the location. Everything was prepared for our big day.

Easter Tuesday, 31 March, 8 am.

A fleet of cars had assembled at the Hotel-Restaurant Schweighofer to take the proprietors and guests to the bride's house in the next village. The ladies looked glamorous in their wedding gowns, the men more solemn in traditional black with white carnation button holes.

'I only hope they won't take me for the head waiter,' Brian had joked at the unusual request for a black wedding suit. One of the few to keep calm on his wedding day, he'd managed to avert yet another dilemma: it was the groom's nimble jeweller's fingers that were called upon when the zip of Aunt Ida's dress hopelessly jammed. From then on everything, well, nearly everything, went like clockwork. Nine o'clock sharp and the convoy, led by the car of bridesmaid and groom and ending with the flower-decked limousine of bride and best man, left 47 Market Square, Rastenfeld, proceeding towards Zwettl.

It was one of those bright, crisp spring mornings. Lake Ottenstein in the Waldviertel's heart had never looked more romantic than seen with the eyes of a bride on her wedding day: crystal clear waters caressed sun-kissed island castles, while mighty forests stood guard at the shore . . . Large crowds had gathered by the Zwettl register office to cheer the local teacher and her English husband-to-be. And here, there, and everywhere Uncle Willi and his camera popped up, recording the whole happy atmosphere.

The civil ceremony completed, the wedding convoy proceeded towards the Stift Zwettl monastery. A chorus of sweet, pure girls' voices echoed from the cloisters as the procession approached the collegiate church. And there they were, 30 beaming little faces welcoming teacher on her wedding day. The door opened to the rousing sound of the organ. The procession parted to form a line of honour. The bride, on the arm of the best man, walked slowly down the aisle to join her groom at the high altar. The wedding service began.

My dear colleagues and pupils had excelled in making our wedding a true bilingual occasion. Chapter by chapter the sermon was translated by Egon while the girls of Three A, conducted by Traute, sang hymns in both German and English. The marriage vows proved easy for Brian. A clear 'Ja!' to the priest's questions was all that was required. When we exchanged rings I couldn't help smiling. Trust Brian to think of an explanation why most Europeans wear the wedding ring on the right hand: 'Could it have to do with driving on the other side of the road?' More hymns, a kiss for the bride and finally the signing of the church register. Then, the radiant new

Our big day.

Mrs. Marshall, at the arm of her smiling husband, led the procession out of the church.

A true perfectionist, my uncle had recorded every detail of the wedding service. However, a touch nervous, he must have turned the film over twice. There was no other explanation for the strange phenomenon of the civil and church ceremony simultaneously happening on a large section of the film.

Poor Willi nearly tore out his hair when later confronted with the fiasco. Fortunately, he wasn't aware of it at the time and happily carried on shooting; so at least the reception turned out unspoilt on the film.

While the leading characters diverted to Studio Lux for their photo session, everyone else went ahead to the Cafe-Restaurant Loidl. My pupils and their choir mistress warmed up with hot chocolate and cakes, the rest with something slightly stronger. Thundering applause greeted the newlyweds on their arrival. After a toast to the bride and groom they led their guests to the reception.

The large dining room of Loidl's restaurant looked fabulous: crisp white damask gracing U-shaped tables, matching serviettes folded into the shapes of doves and magnificent floral decorations everywhere. But it was the unusual two-tier wedding cake, the centre-piece of the table, that stole the show. Baked by Brian's mother, it had travelled all the way from England in the groom's car.

'There is also a bit of my handiwork in that cake,' my new husband stated proudly.

'You clever thing! I didn't know cake decorating was your forte.'

'It isn't,' Brian grinned. 'We left that to the professionals. But I'm well pleased with my repair job. You see, once when I had to brake hard on the journey the cake box shot off the back seat and some of the icing got broken. Managed to mend the curly bits with white cardboard. You won't tell Mother, promise!' I promised and nobody seemed to notice.

Floral place cards dedicated one wing of the table to the English guests and everyone who could speak their language.

It was from there where all the laughter came when telegrams were read, speeches delivered and toasts given. The Anglo-Austrian wedding feast seemed to go down extremely well. When it was time for cutting the cake everyone's eyes were upon us.

'Beware of the cardboard bits!' Brian hissed during our first symbolic act as a married couple.

Yet the rapture turned into disbelief when the cake, whisked away by Mrs. Tinnion, reappeared in matchbox sized pieces on everyone's plate. My fellow-countrymen were unfamiliar with the strange custom of saving most of the wedding cake for absent friends and even for the first christening. They also have good appetites and enjoy their pastries in generous portions. Consequently, Mrs. Tinnion's kindly gesture earned her the reputation of being rather stingy.

With the formal part of the reception over, the guests began to mingle. Brian pointed to our two mums who, with Traute's help, were engaged in intense conversation. I could guess what it was all about: Mama pleading with Mrs. Marshall to take her daughter under her wings. I also knew that my dear mother-in-law would honour her promise as long as she lived. It was late afternoon when the English guests left with the Trappls for a holiday in Vienna. With the rest of the party still in full swing, Brian and I slipped away to start our honeymoon.

A room under the name of Marshall had been reserved at a Krems Hotel for weeks. It was the name 'Weisse Rose' (The White Rose) which had made me choose it for our first night.

The next day the new Mr. and Mrs. Marshall headed south via Carinthia reaching their honeymoon destination on 2 April. To me the spa town of Meran looked even more enchanting than on my 1957 visit with Omi: majestic snow-capped mountains clearly defined against a cloudless sky and wonderful parks, gardens and promenades blooming with Forsythia, Japanese Cherry and Magnolia. Forsythia was a spiky shrub, leafless, just one mass of golden bells, Magnolia, Brian's favourite, a tall standard tree with huge tulip-blossoms in white or cerise.

Our hotel, the Pension Andreas Hofer on Meran's outskirts, offered everything one could wish for: breathtaking views over the valley and the mountains, spotless, well appointed rooms and good solid Austrian cooking. We were surprised and delighted to be welcomed with flowers, champagne and books of complimentary tickets for the town's main attractions. The local tourist office ran this promotion to attract off-season guests, especially honeymoon couples, we learned. This, however, had one drawback: instant recognition as newly-weds not only at the Andreas Hofer, but anywhere else in Meran. It was my cousin Anneliese we had to thank for this unwelcome blaze of publicity!

Another source of embarrassment was our landlady, Frau Huber. One of the second generation of staunch Austrians under 'foreign' rule, she made no secret of her dislike of the Italians or, indeed, any 'out-lander'. Although sympathetic to me, the 'poor, misguided soul', she completely ignored 'that Englishman husband of hers' who couldn't even speak German!

'Guten Morgen, Frau Marshall! Gut geschlafen? Ahhhh' was her daily catch-phrase when Brian and I appeared at the breakfast table.

These unforgettable words of our Italian landlady, perfectly copied by my dear husband, would often generate our first laugh on the grey English mornings to come.

To escape the prying eyes at the Andreas Hofer Brian and I embarked on daily marathon walks. There was a good reason for not using the car:

'Don't fancy having Father's vehicle rammed by some mad Italian driver!' Only once could my car enthusiast husband be persuaded to drive. Lake Garda was just too long a walk from the Pension Andreas Hofer. But who needed a car in a romantic place like Meran? Using our honeymoon tickets on chair lifts and cable cars, we would frequently head for the mountains. And what better place than an open-air café for a meal with the most spectacular panoramic views thrown in?

However, pasta, pizza and vino frequently disagreed with my husband's conservative English stomach, and to this day he dislikes Italian food.

To have a few more days with my parents before leaving for England we decided to cut short our honeymoon and take a more direct route home. But one diversion was required to collect our surprise present for Papa. The kennel, recommended by dog-loving Pfarrer Wiesinger, was not easy to find in a big industrial city like Linz but we got there in the end. Viewing the latest litter of Alsatians, we learned that all dog puppies were sold. But we both fell for bright-eyed, floppy-eared black-and-tan Susi (kennel name 'Susanne von der Falknerklause') with an arm-long pedigree. To ease Susi's distress over leaving her mother Brian suggested I should sit with her in the back. The rear seat of the car was less cramped and covered with paper, just in case. But all the way to Rastenfeld the little dog never moved.

'I hope she's still alive,' Brian kept saying. His attention diverted from the city traffic, he once found himself in the wrong lane, narrowly missing another car. The other driver went spare over what could have happened: 'Brainless foreigners! Come here and show no regard for our people and traffic!' On and on he went until the lights changed to amber. Then a mighty roar of his engine and, still gesticulating, he disappeared in a cloud of blue smoke. The Engishman's wife in the other car hadn't let on she'd understood every word of Mr. Angry's barrage. There are times when it pays to appear ignorant.

My parents couldn't believe their eyes to see us arrive early with an Alsatian puppy in tow. Papa, of course, was in raptures over Susi who, once released from the car, had come back to life. Mama pretended likewise not to hurt our feelings. It was all the fuss over Susi that helped relieve tensions and made our last days in Rastenfeld really happy.

Finally, the day arrived when I had to say goodbye to my loved ones. A few tears on both sides, a last hug, kiss and wave and the British car, packed with countless gifts and memories, left the Austrian village. There was one more stop: the cemetery on the outskirts. I couldn't have gone away without saying goodbye to my grandma. All my life I had turned to Omi when I felt sad. The stories she told always had happy endings. How did the one go which was my declared favourite? 'She followed her prince to a foreign land and they lived happily ever after . . .'

Gradually, a great calm came over me. The future in a strange country bore no more threat. This was my bit to promote understanding and peace among peoples.

'Let other nations fight the wars,' the emperor Maximilian's famous words rang into Brian's startled ears. 'You, happy Austria, marry!'

EPILOGUE

It is 1992. The car with the British registration has turned off the busy new by-pass, threaded its way through the narrow village street and finally stopped at the cemetery on Rastenfeld's outskirts.

'Shan't be long, Brian. Just plant the rose on our grave.'

He nods, turns off the engine and helps his wife retrieve the white rose bush from the boot. He makes no attempt to follow her, sensing her need to be alone with her loved ones and her memories.

He watches as the wrought-iron gate closes behind her with a creak. Slowly she walks between the graves ablaze with autumn flowers heading for the tombstone inscribed with all those precious family names: Franziska Tesch, Minna Schweighofer, Franz Tesch, Ernst Schweighofer.

Tears prick her eyes as she reflects on her mother's untimely death so soon after her own move to England, and Papa's devastation and loneliness over his great loss. She thinks of dear old Opa who had followed his daughter three years later and of her beloved Omi who'd left the family long ago.

She recalls the last time she'd stood at this graveside. That was in 1981 at her father's funeral, and she hasn't been back since. Papa's second wife, Herma, a family friend from Vienna, had been warm and welcoming at first. But later her jealousy and deteriorating health made her more and more intolerant towards her step-daughter and her offspring. Also, Aunt Herma's bad rapport with old village friends had caused friction between them and spoilt their relationship. Their home-visits became less frequent and stopped altogether when Papa died and the house was sold to pay for Aunt Hermia's nursing care.

Now, with her sons grown up and away from home, she'd felt the urge to see her homeland Austria again, and Rastenfeld, the place of her childhood, was an essential part of this sentimental journey.

'You'll be surprised how tourism has transformed the Waldviertel during your absence,' her cousin Karl from neighbouring Friedersbach had warned them. 'It's caused quite a turn-around in village life.' His fabulous hotel and conference complex where they had booked in, confirmed his words.

At first they had noticed little difference from the Rastenfeld of yesteryear. The old church with the slender steeple had stubbornly defied all modern change and St. Florian still guarded the village square. But what on earth had happened to the house opposite that fountain, the home of her childhood and youth? The bright pink-facade clashed with the new red roof tiles and the gleaming PVC windows looked all wrong against the grey stone base of the house. Deprived of their lace curtains and flower boxes, they appeared naked and bare. Gone were the two lovely feathery trees and the seat they had shaded. Gone, too, the ornamental sign pronouncing this house a family builder's residence since 1908. But then, the business had been dissolved years ago and no-one called Tesch or Schweighofer lived here any more. The only place to bear those well-known names now was a tombstone of grey marble.

As she plants the white rose tree on the family grave she lets her tears flow freely. An elderly woman approaches from behind, interrupting her thoughts and prayer.

'I can't believe it! Am I seeing right? It's Jutta, our dear Jutta!' Anni Österreicher's kind, weather-beaten face lights up under the dark head scarf and two rough farmer's hands extend towards her.

'Welcome home, Jutta! It's been such a long time! Wait till I tell Rudi, Elli and the family. You'll come and see us, won't you? Will tomorrow be alright? And Jutta, you must pop into Brandtner's shop. Ulli would never forgive herself if she'd missed you this time!'

In the old friend's warm embrace, her misery and sadness instantly melt away.

'God bless you, Anni! Can't tell you how good it is to be home again. Just let me warn my long-suffering Brian he's got a lot more visiting to endure. There is so much catching up to do on old times before I can go back to England . . .